TABLE OF CONTENTS

TABLE OF CONTENTS

#	SUBJECT	PAGE

TABLE OF CONTENTS

#	SUBJECT	PAGE

YEARLY PAYMENTS & DEPOSITS

YEAR : ....

MONTH	PAYMENT / DEBIT (-)	DEPOSIT / CREDIT (+)	BALANCE	NOTES
TOTAL				

NOTES

YEARLY PAYMENTS & DEPOSITS CHART

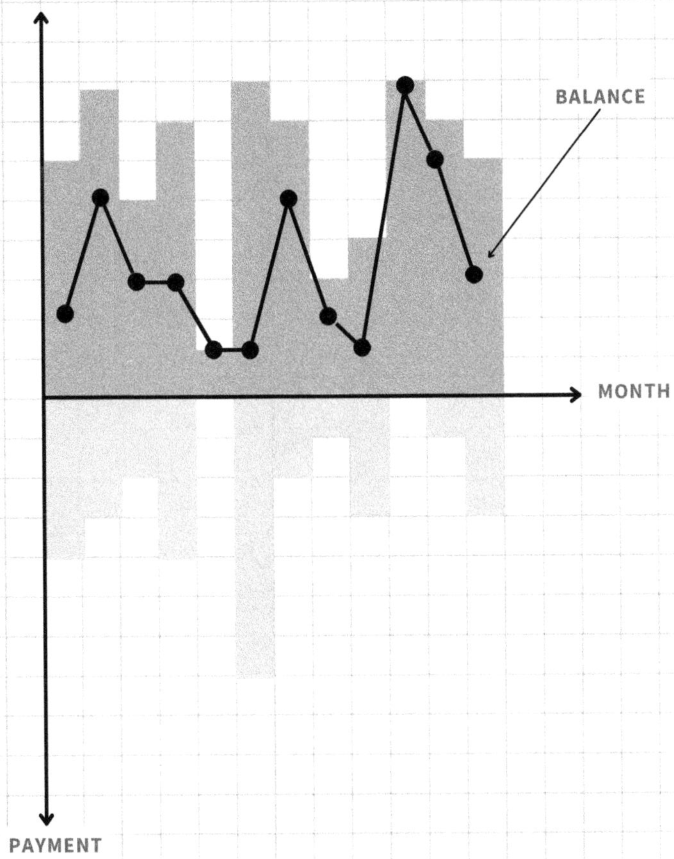

HOW TO:

BUILD YOUR CHART USING YOUR MONTHLY PAYMENTS & DEPOSITS SUMMARIES:

- CALCULATE YOUR SCALE USING THE HIGHEST NUMBER IN TERMS OF DEPOSIT OR PAYMENT PER MONTH AND DIVIDE IT BY 10 TO GET THE SIZE OF A SQUARE ON THE Y AXIS
- PLOT YOUR TOTAL MONTHLY DEPOSITS AS POSITIVE BARS ON THE Y-AXIS AND YOUR TOTAL MONTHLY PAYMENTS AS NEGATIVE BARS ON THE Y-AXIS (DIVIDE MONTHLY DEPOSIT/PAYMENT BY THE SIZE OF A SQUARE TO FIND THE NUMBER OF SQUARES TO FILL)
- BUILD YOUR BALANCE LINE CHART USING YOUR MONTHLY BALANCE

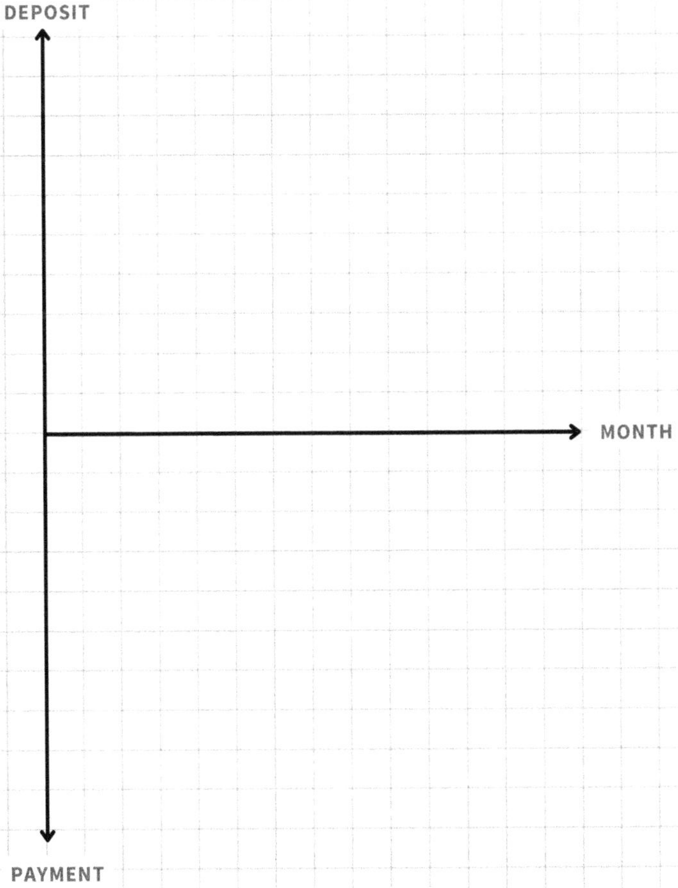

YEAR:

NOTES:

MONTHLY PAYMENTS & DEPOSITS

MONTH : ....

DATE	DAY	PAYMENT / DEBIT (-)	DEPOSIT / CREDIT (+)	BALANCE	NOTES
1					
2					
3					
4					
5					
6					
7					
8					
9					
10					
11					
12					
13					
14					
15					
16					
17					
18					
19					
20					
21					
22					
23					
24					
25					
26					
27					
28					
29					
30					
31					
TOTAL					

MONTHLY PAYMENTS & DEPOSITS CHART

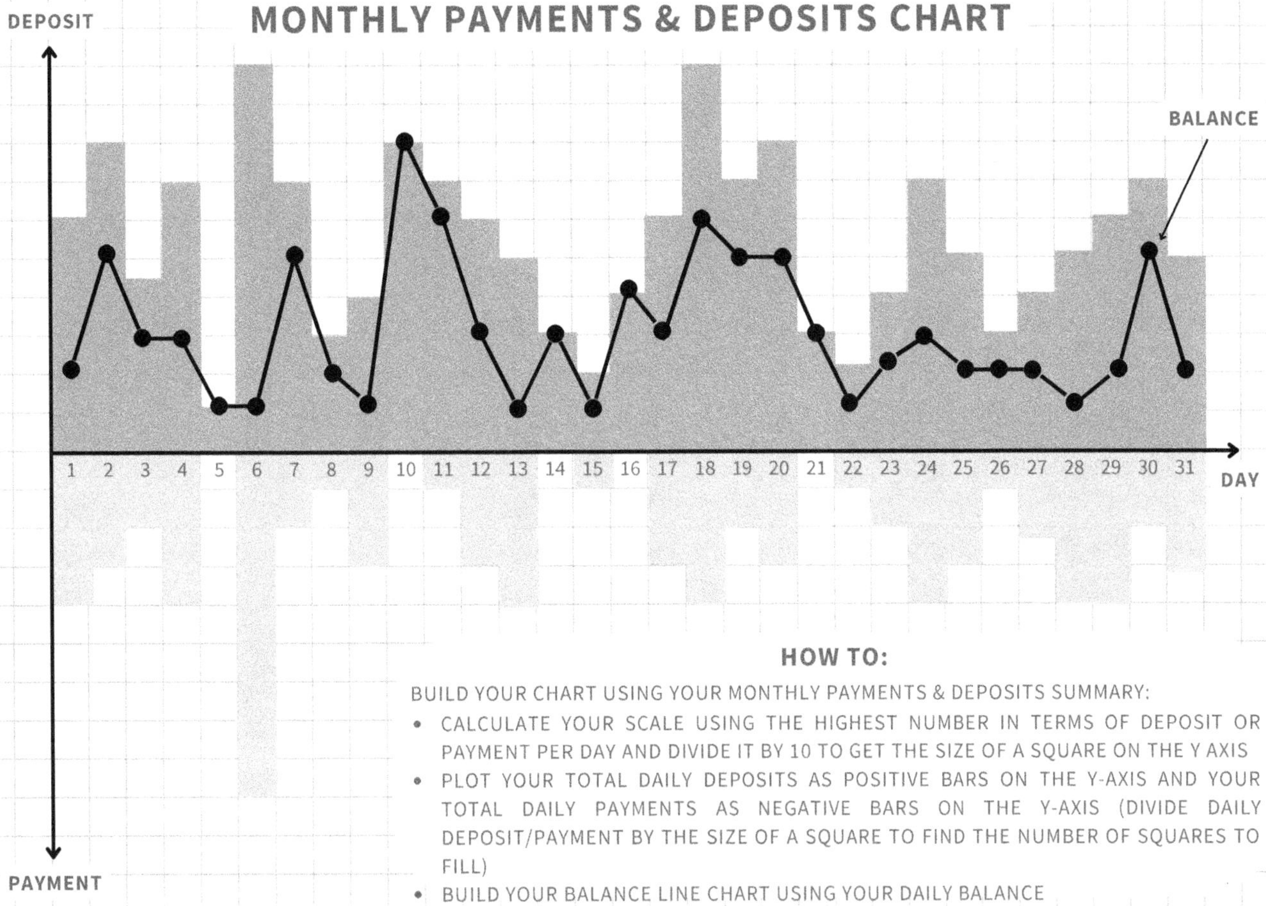

HOW TO:

BUILD YOUR CHART USING YOUR MONTHLY PAYMENTS & DEPOSITS SUMMARY:

- CALCULATE YOUR SCALE USING THE HIGHEST NUMBER IN TERMS OF DEPOSIT OR PAYMENT PER DAY AND DIVIDE IT BY 10 TO GET THE SIZE OF A SQUARE ON THE Y AXIS
- PLOT YOUR TOTAL DAILY DEPOSITS AS POSITIVE BARS ON THE Y-AXIS AND YOUR TOTAL DAILY PAYMENTS AS NEGATIVE BARS ON THE Y-AXIS (DIVIDE DAILY DEPOSIT/PAYMENT BY THE SIZE OF A SQUARE TO FIND THE NUMBER OF SQUARES TO FILL)
- BUILD YOUR BALANCE LINE CHART USING YOUR DAILY BALANCE

MONTH:

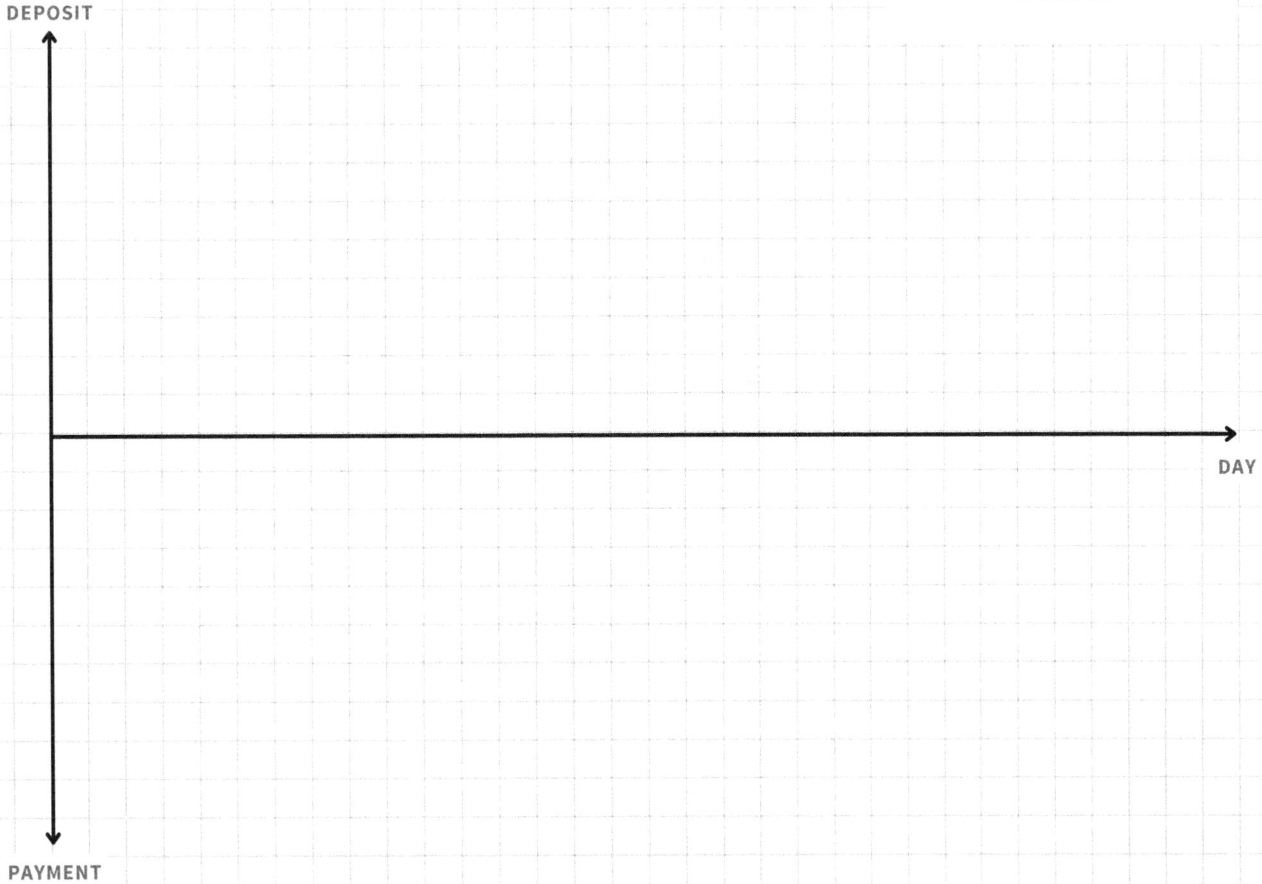

MONTHLY PAYMENTS & DEPOSITS

MONTH : ....

DATE	DAY	PAYMENT / DEBIT (-)	DEPOSIT / CREDIT (+)	BALANCE	NOTES
1					
2					
3					
4					
5					
6					
7					
8					
9					
10					
11					
12					
13					
14					
15					
16					
17					
18					
19					
20					
21					
22					
23					
24					
25					
26					
27					
28					
29					
30					
31					
TOTAL					

MONTHLY PAYMENTS & DEPOSITS CHART

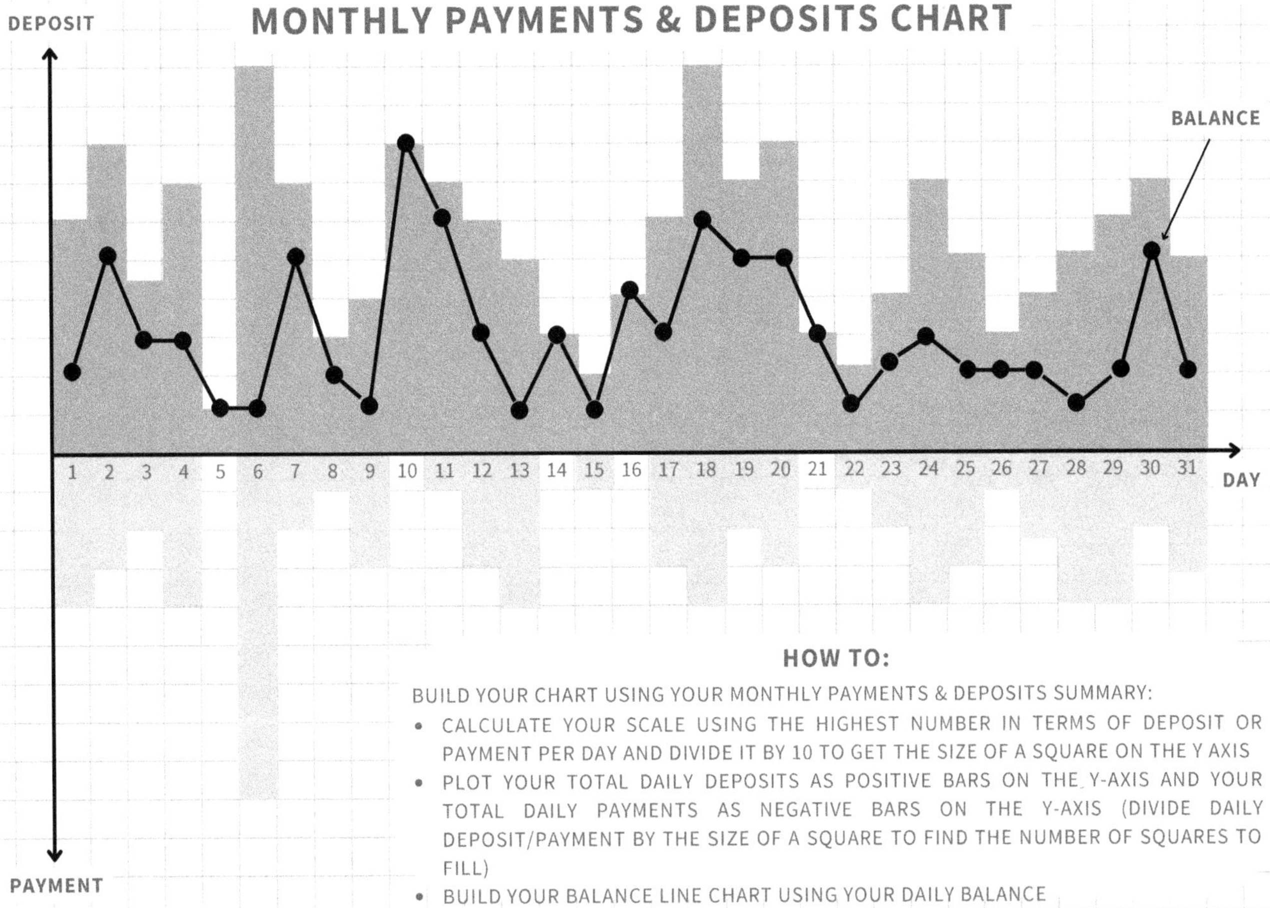

HOW TO:

BUILD YOUR CHART USING YOUR MONTHLY PAYMENTS & DEPOSITS SUMMARY:

- CALCULATE YOUR SCALE USING THE HIGHEST NUMBER IN TERMS OF DEPOSIT OR PAYMENT PER DAY AND DIVIDE IT BY 10 TO GET THE SIZE OF A SQUARE ON THE Y AXIS
- PLOT YOUR TOTAL DAILY DEPOSITS AS POSITIVE BARS ON THE Y-AXIS AND YOUR TOTAL DAILY PAYMENTS AS NEGATIVE BARS ON THE Y-AXIS (DIVIDE DAILY DEPOSIT/PAYMENT BY THE SIZE OF A SQUARE TO FIND THE NUMBER OF SQUARES TO FILL)
- BUILD YOUR BALANCE LINE CHART USING YOUR DAILY BALANCE

MONTH:

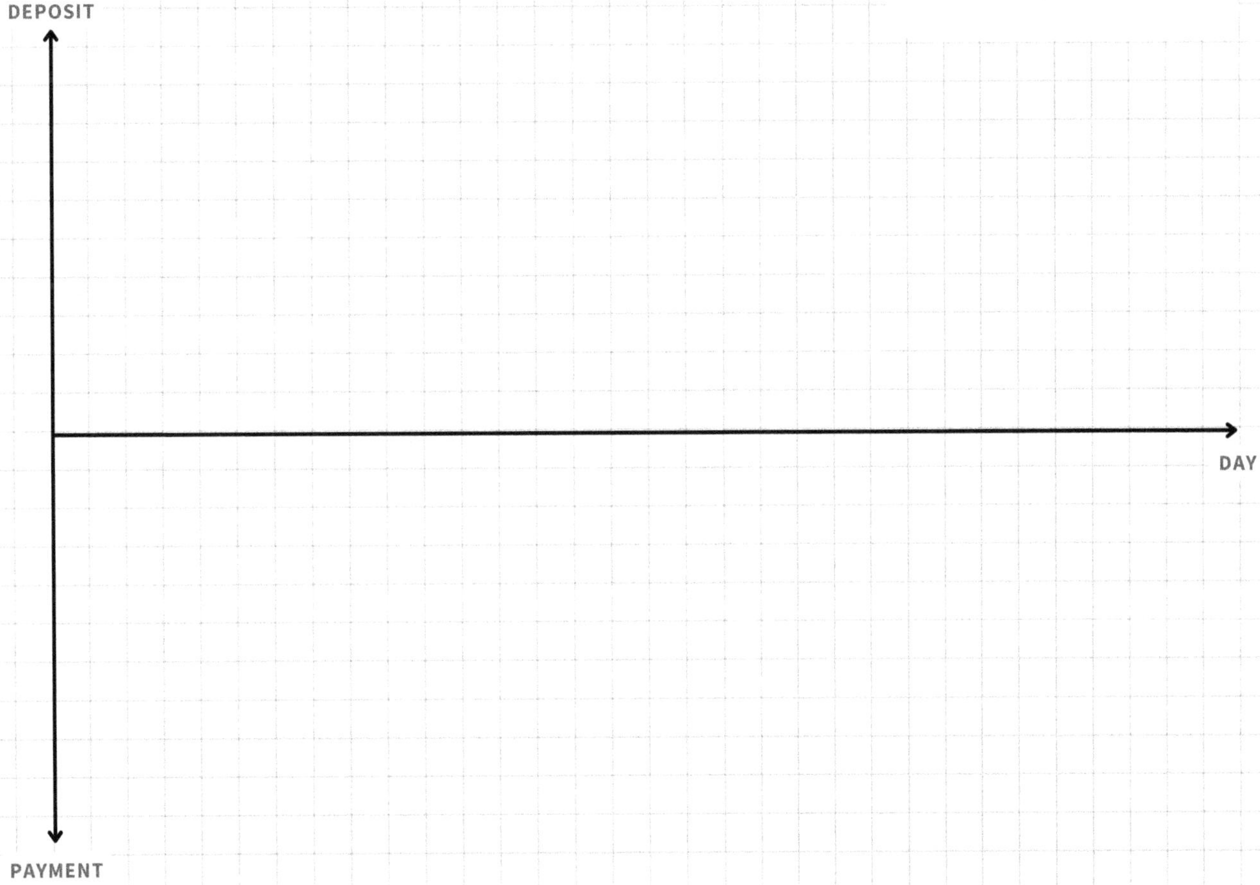

MONTHLY PAYMENTS & DEPOSITS

MONTH : ....

DATE	DAY	PAYMENT / DEBIT (-)	DEPOSIT / CREDIT (+)	BALANCE	NOTES
1					
2					
3					
4					
5					
6					
7					
8					
9					
10					
11					
12					
13					
14					
15					
16					
17					
18					
19					
20					
21					
22					
23					
24					
25					
26					
27					
28					
29					
30					
31					
TOTAL					

MONTHLY PAYMENTS & DEPOSITS CHART

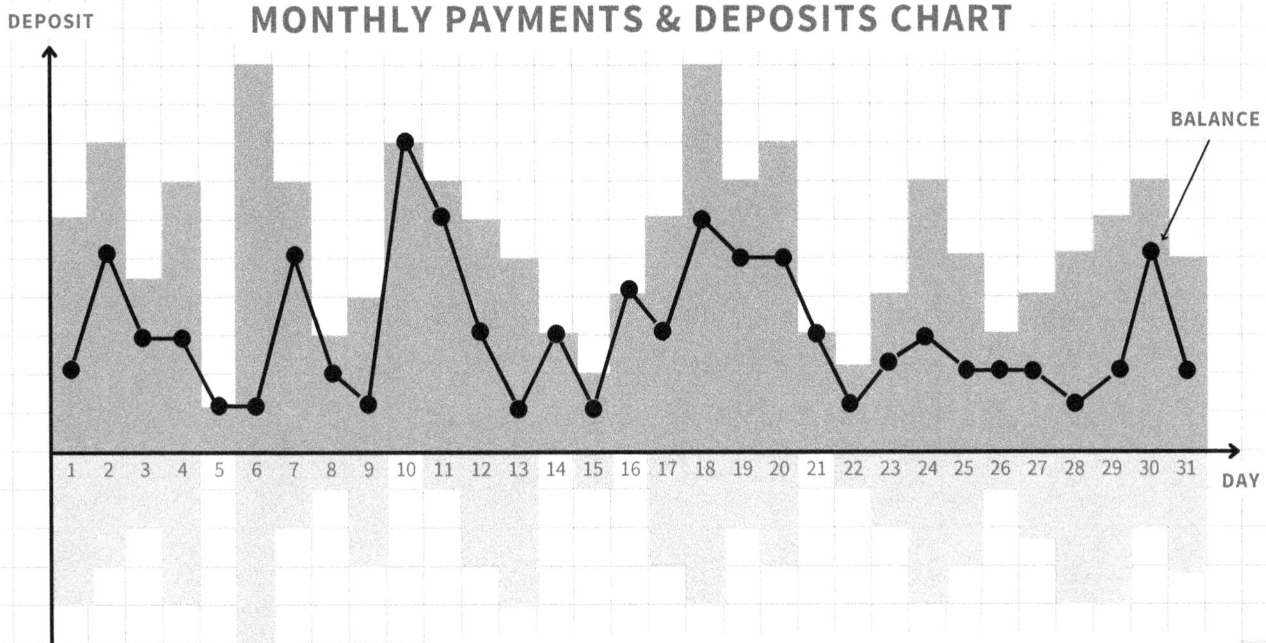

HOW TO:

BUILD YOUR CHART USING YOUR MONTHLY PAYMENTS & DEPOSITS SUMMARY:

- CALCULATE YOUR SCALE USING THE HIGHEST NUMBER IN TERMS OF DEPOSIT OR PAYMENT PER DAY AND DIVIDE IT BY 10 TO GET THE SIZE OF A SQUARE ON THE Y AXIS
- PLOT YOUR TOTAL DAILY DEPOSITS AS POSITIVE BARS ON THE Y-AXIS AND YOUR TOTAL DAILY PAYMENTS AS NEGATIVE BARS ON THE Y-AXIS (DIVIDE DAILY DEPOSIT/PAYMENT BY THE SIZE OF A SQUARE TO FIND THE NUMBER OF SQUARES TO FILL)
- BUILD YOUR BALANCE LINE CHART USING YOUR DAILY BALANCE

MONTH:

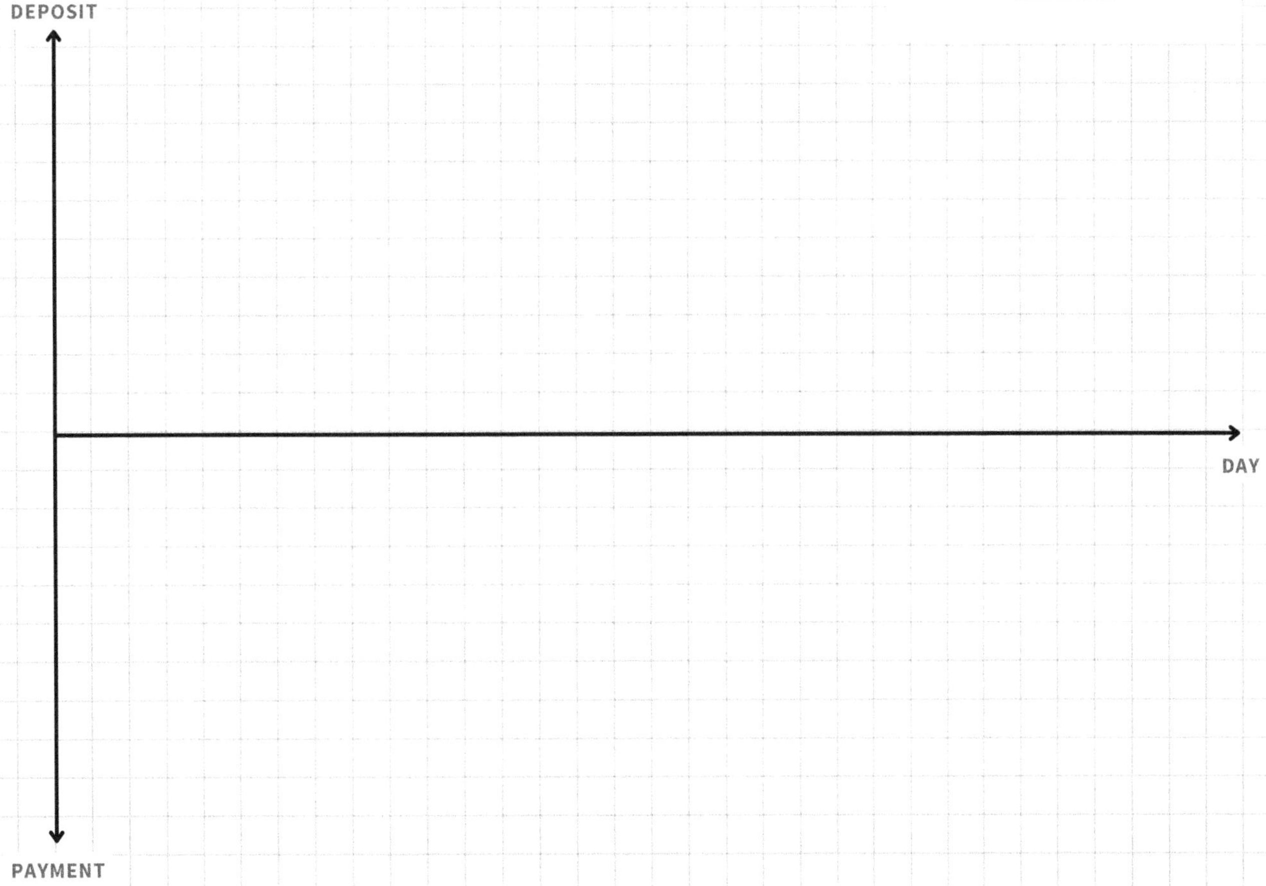

MONTHLY PAYMENTS & DEPOSITS

MONTH : ....

DATE	DAY	PAYMENT / DEBIT (-)	DEPOSIT / CREDIT (+)	BALANCE	NOTES
1					
2					
3					
4					
5					
6					
7					
8					
9					
10					
11					
12					
13					
14					
15					
16					
17					
18					
19					
20					
21					
22					
23					
24					
25					
26					
27					
28					
29					
30					
31					
TOTAL					

MONTHLY PAYMENTS & DEPOSITS CHART

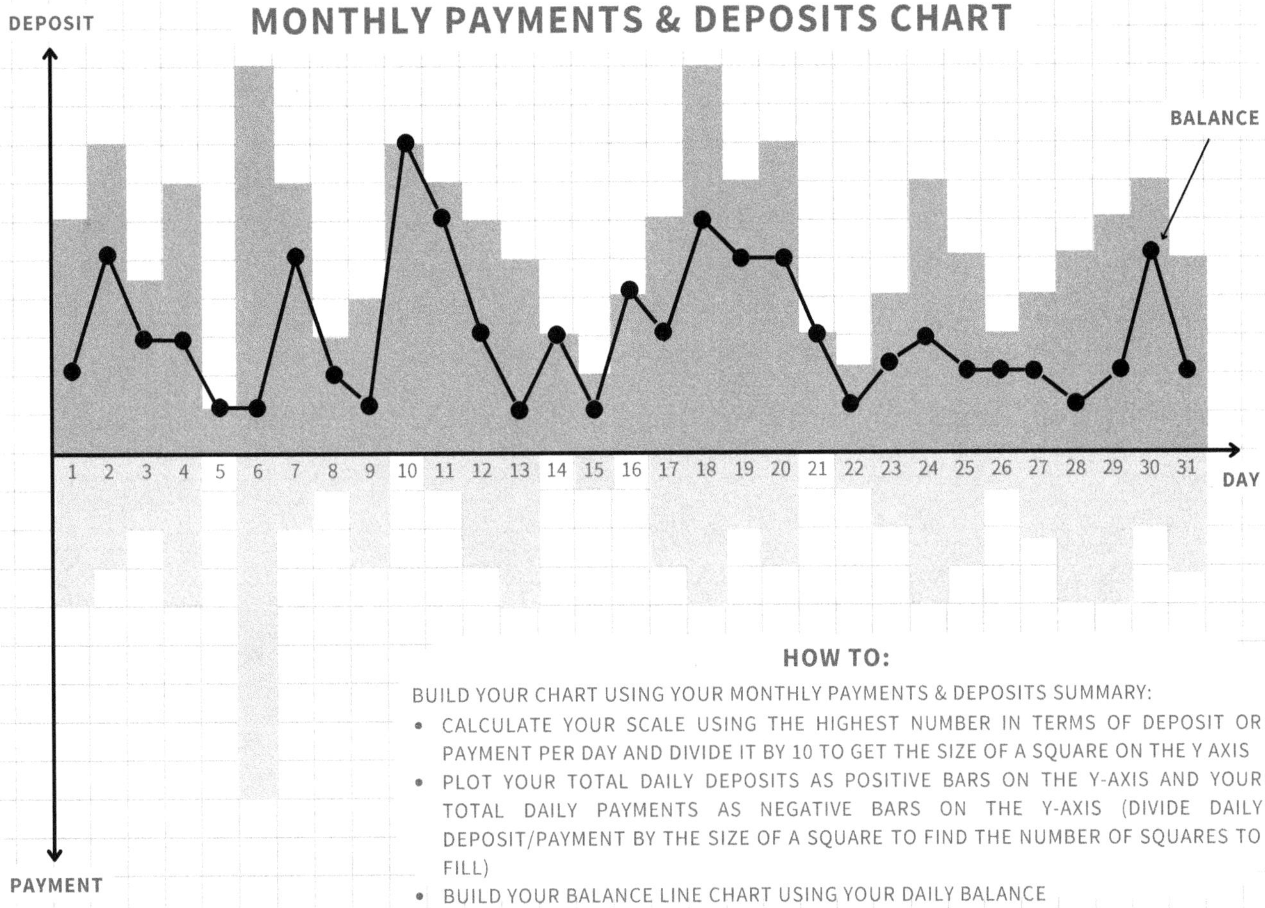

HOW TO:

BUILD YOUR CHART USING YOUR MONTHLY PAYMENTS & DEPOSITS SUMMARY:

- CALCULATE YOUR SCALE USING THE HIGHEST NUMBER IN TERMS OF DEPOSIT OR PAYMENT PER DAY AND DIVIDE IT BY 10 TO GET THE SIZE OF A SQUARE ON THE Y AXIS
- PLOT YOUR TOTAL DAILY DEPOSITS AS POSITIVE BARS ON THE Y-AXIS AND YOUR TOTAL DAILY PAYMENTS AS NEGATIVE BARS ON THE Y-AXIS (DIVIDE DAILY DEPOSIT/PAYMENT BY THE SIZE OF A SQUARE TO FIND THE NUMBER OF SQUARES TO FILL)
- BUILD YOUR BALANCE LINE CHART USING YOUR DAILY BALANCE

MONTH:

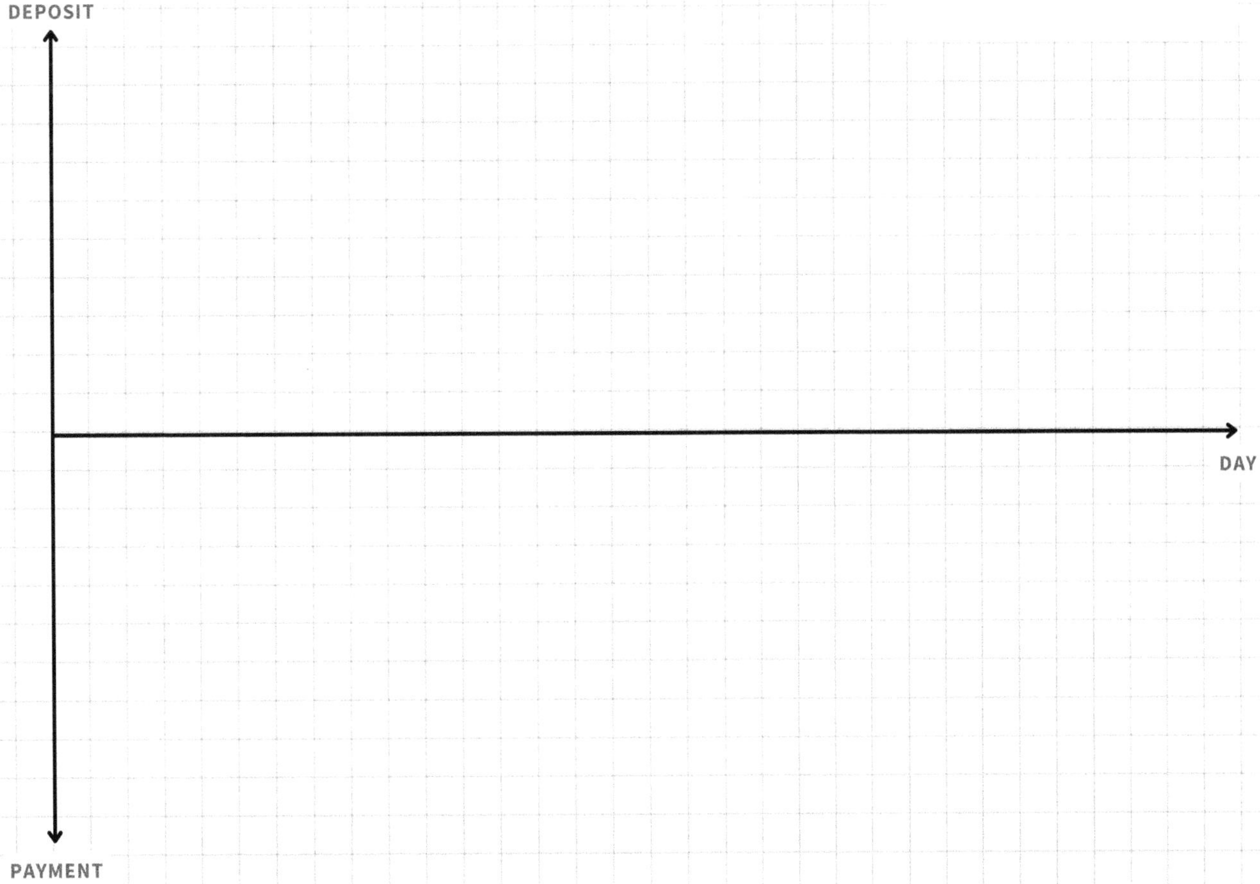

MONTHLY PAYMENTS & DEPOSITS

MONTH : ....

DATE	DAY	PAYMENT / DEBIT (-)	DEPOSIT / CREDIT (+)	BALANCE	NOTES
1					
2					
3					
4					
5					
6					
7					
8					
9					
10					
11					
12					
13					
14					
15					
16					
17					
18					
19					
20					
21					
22					
23					
24					
25					
26					
27					
28					
29					
30					
31					
TOTAL					

MONTHLY PAYMENTS & DEPOSITS CHART

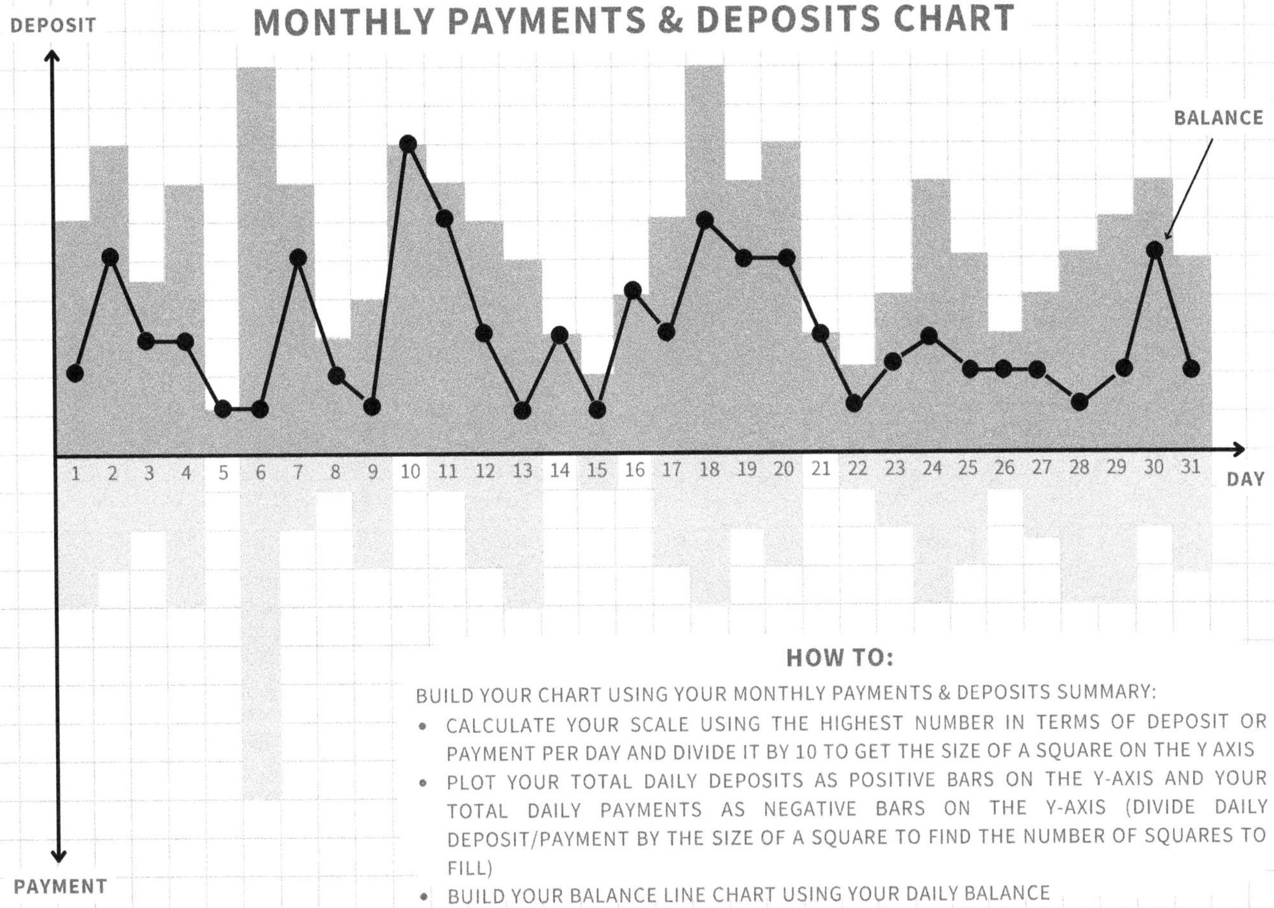

HOW TO:

BUILD YOUR CHART USING YOUR MONTHLY PAYMENTS & DEPOSITS SUMMARY:

- CALCULATE YOUR SCALE USING THE HIGHEST NUMBER IN TERMS OF DEPOSIT OR PAYMENT PER DAY AND DIVIDE IT BY 10 TO GET THE SIZE OF A SQUARE ON THE Y AXIS
- PLOT YOUR TOTAL DAILY DEPOSITS AS POSITIVE BARS ON THE Y-AXIS AND YOUR TOTAL DAILY PAYMENTS AS NEGATIVE BARS ON THE Y-AXIS (DIVIDE DAILY DEPOSIT/PAYMENT BY THE SIZE OF A SQUARE TO FIND THE NUMBER OF SQUARES TO FILL)
- BUILD YOUR BALANCE LINE CHART USING YOUR DAILY BALANCE

MONTH:

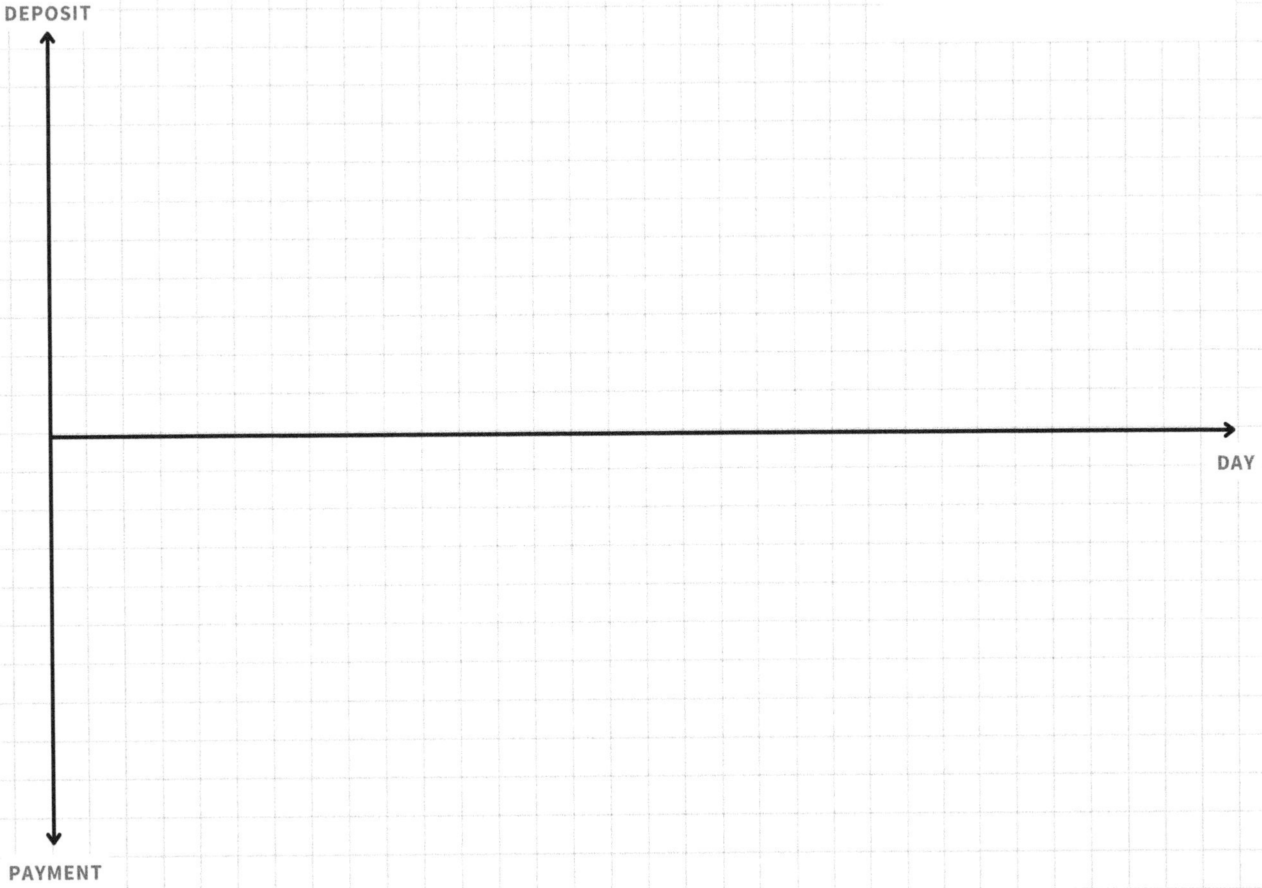

MONTHLY PAYMENTS & DEPOSITS

MONTH : ....

DATE	DAY	PAYMENT / DEBIT (-)	DEPOSIT / CREDIT (+)	BALANCE	NOTES
1					
2					
3					
4					
5					
6					
7					
8					
9					
10					
11					
12					
13					
14					
15					
16					
17					
18					
19					
20					
21					
22					
23					
24					
25					
26					
27					
28					
29					
30					
31					
TOTAL					

MONTHLY PAYMENTS & DEPOSITS CHART

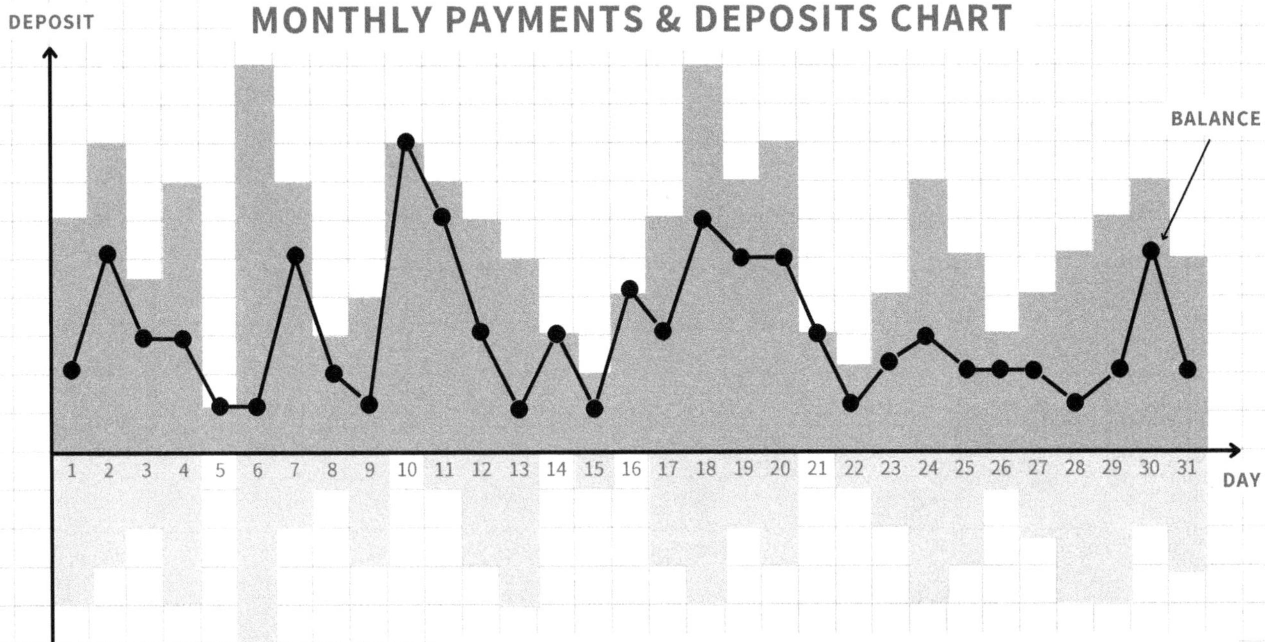

HOW TO:

BUILD YOUR CHART USING YOUR MONTHLY PAYMENTS & DEPOSITS SUMMARY:

- CALCULATE YOUR SCALE USING THE HIGHEST NUMBER IN TERMS OF DEPOSIT OR PAYMENT PER DAY AND DIVIDE IT BY 10 TO GET THE SIZE OF A SQUARE ON THE Y AXIS
- PLOT YOUR TOTAL DAILY DEPOSITS AS POSITIVE BARS ON THE Y-AXIS AND YOUR TOTAL DAILY PAYMENTS AS NEGATIVE BARS ON THE Y-AXIS (DIVIDE DAILY DEPOSIT/PAYMENT BY THE SIZE OF A SQUARE TO FIND THE NUMBER OF SQUARES TO FILL)
- BUILD YOUR BALANCE LINE CHART USING YOUR DAILY BALANCE

MONTH:

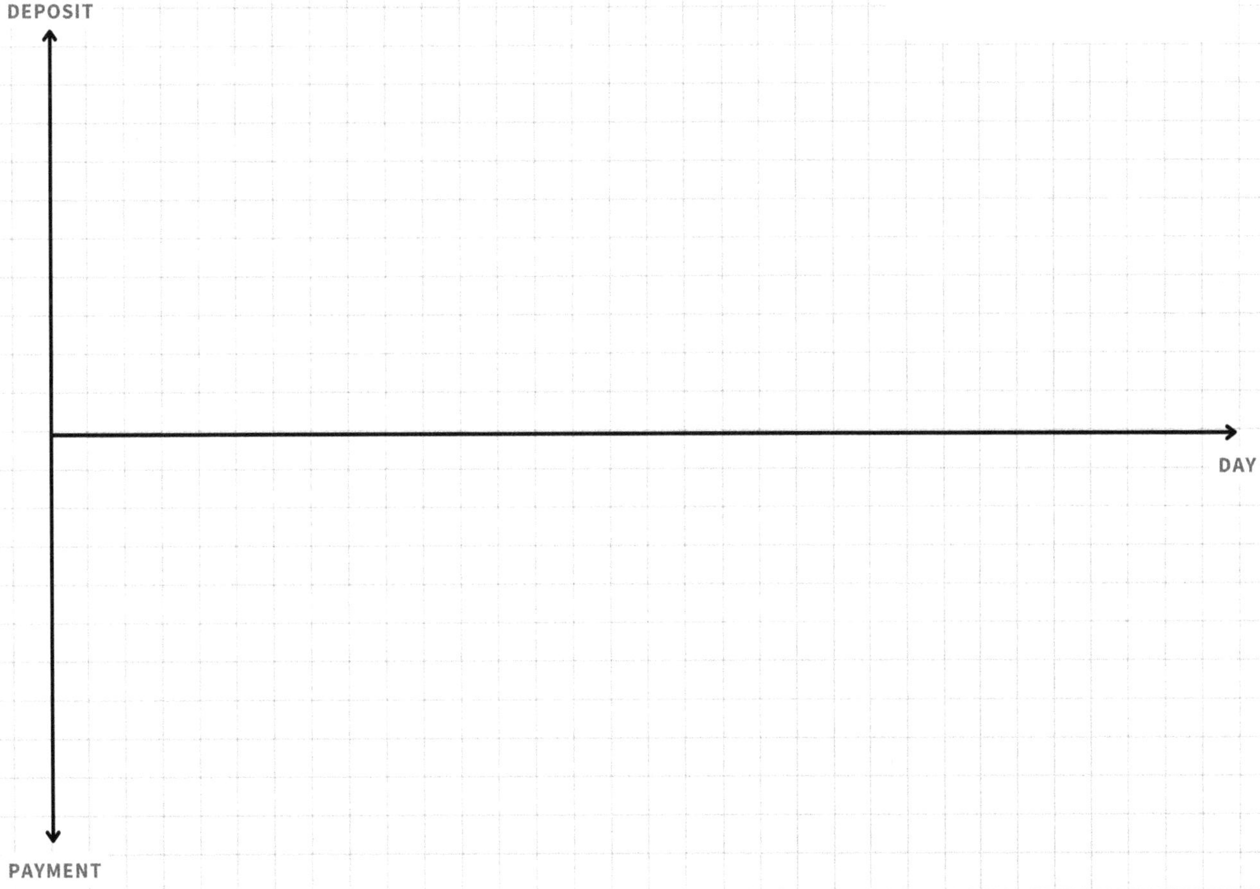

MONTHLY PAYMENTS & DEPOSITS

MONTH : ....

DATE	DAY	PAYMENT / DEBIT (-)	DEPOSIT / CREDIT (+)	BALANCE	NOTES
1					
2					
3					
4					
5					
6					
7					
8					
9					
10					
11					
12					
13					
14					
15					
16					
17					
18					
19					
20					
21					
22					
23					
24					
25					
26					
27					
28					
29					
30					
31					
TOTAL					

MONTHLY PAYMENTS & DEPOSITS CHART

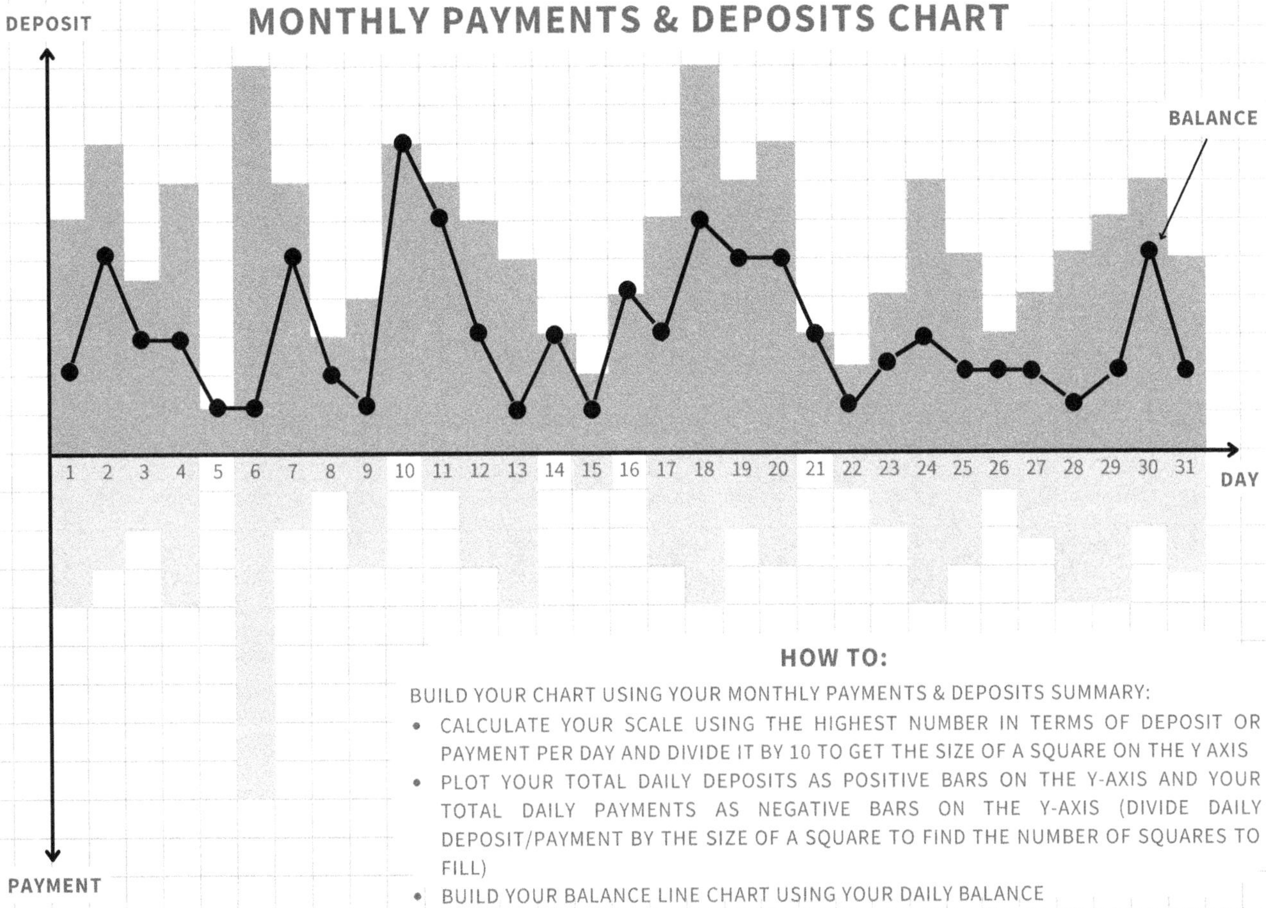

HOW TO:

BUILD YOUR CHART USING YOUR MONTHLY PAYMENTS & DEPOSITS SUMMARY:

- CALCULATE YOUR SCALE USING THE HIGHEST NUMBER IN TERMS OF DEPOSIT OR PAYMENT PER DAY AND DIVIDE IT BY 10 TO GET THE SIZE OF A SQUARE ON THE Y AXIS
- PLOT YOUR TOTAL DAILY DEPOSITS AS POSITIVE BARS ON THE Y-AXIS AND YOUR TOTAL DAILY PAYMENTS AS NEGATIVE BARS ON THE Y-AXIS (DIVIDE DAILY DEPOSIT/PAYMENT BY THE SIZE OF A SQUARE TO FIND THE NUMBER OF SQUARES TO FILL)
- BUILD YOUR BALANCE LINE CHART USING YOUR DAILY BALANCE

MONTH:

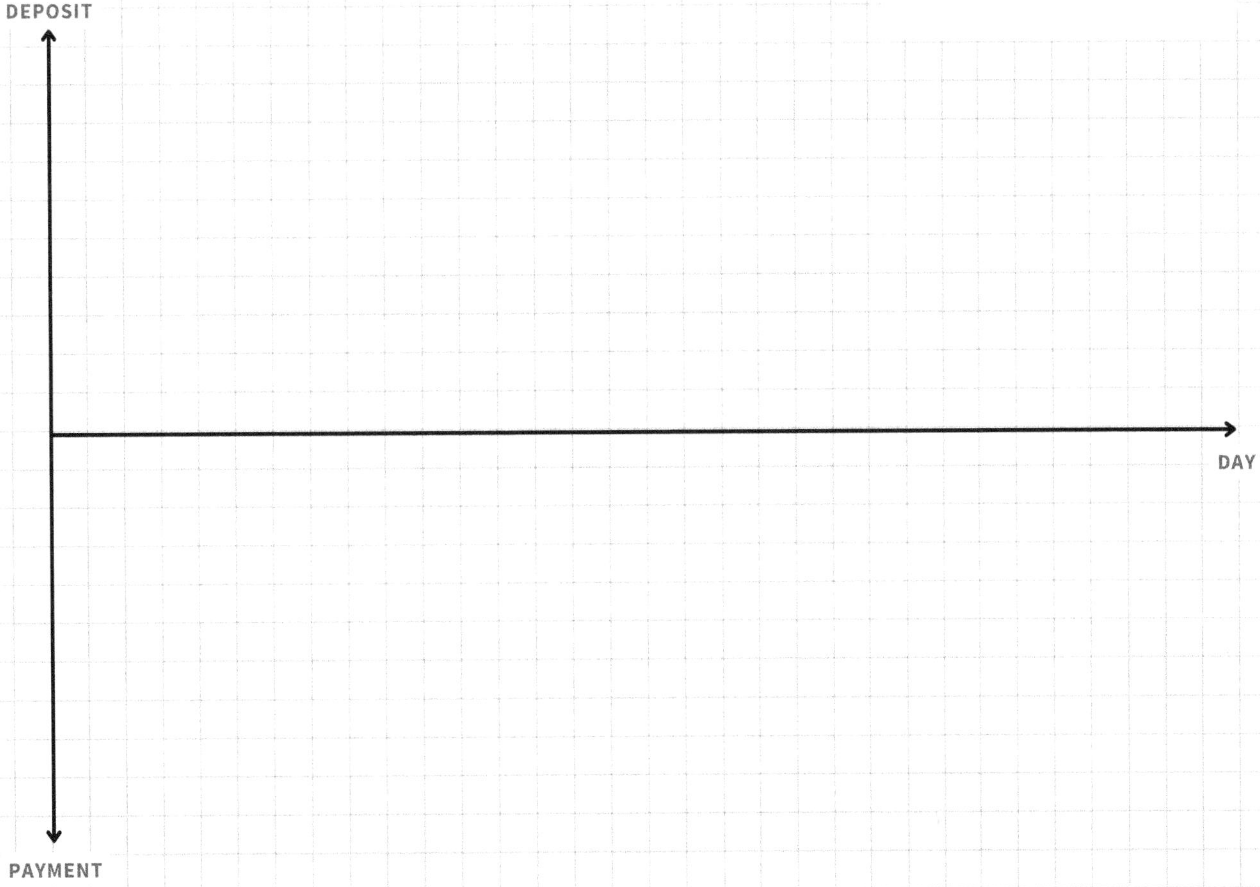

MONTHLY PAYMENTS & DEPOSITS

MONTH : ....

DATE	DAY	PAYMENT / DEBIT (-)	DEPOSIT / CREDIT (+)	BALANCE	NOTES
1					
2					
3					
4					
5					
6					
7					
8					
9					
10					
11					
12					
13					
14					
15					
16					
17					
18					
19					
20					
21					
22					
23					
24					
25					
26					
27					
28					
29					
30					
31					
TOTAL					

MONTHLY PAYMENTS & DEPOSITS CHART

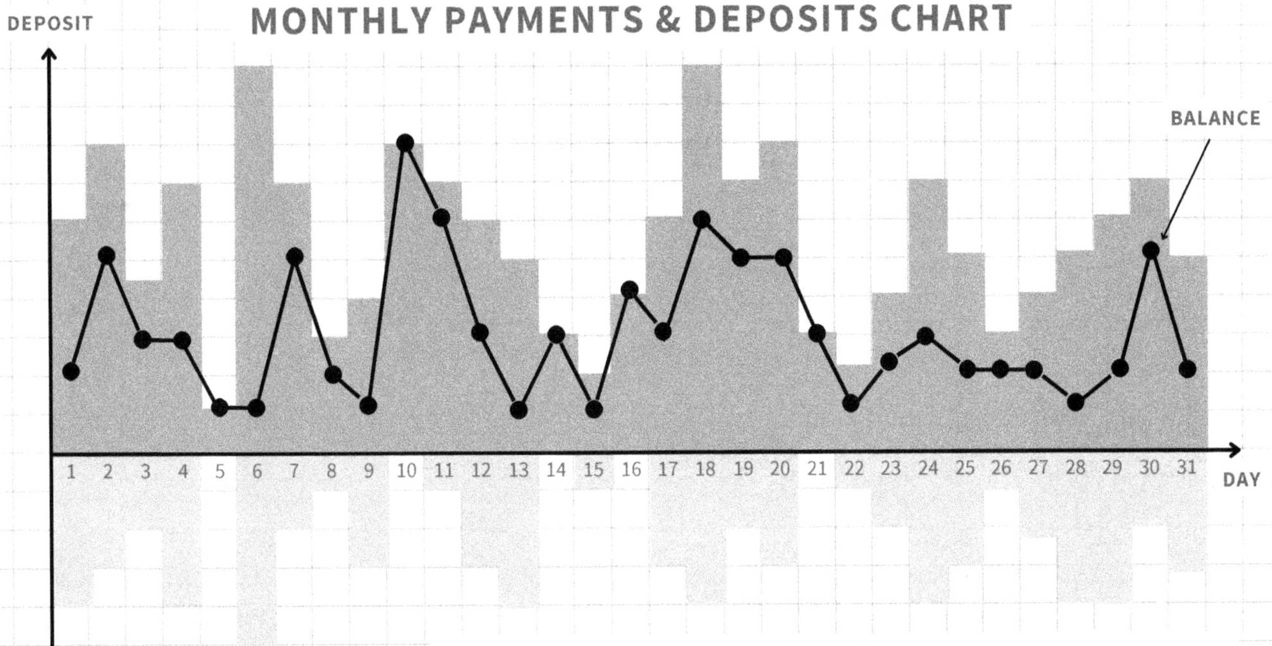

HOW TO:

BUILD YOUR CHART USING YOUR MONTHLY PAYMENTS & DEPOSITS SUMMARY:

- CALCULATE YOUR SCALE USING THE HIGHEST NUMBER IN TERMS OF DEPOSIT OR PAYMENT PER DAY AND DIVIDE IT BY 10 TO GET THE SIZE OF A SQUARE ON THE Y AXIS
- PLOT YOUR TOTAL DAILY DEPOSITS AS POSITIVE BARS ON THE Y-AXIS AND YOUR TOTAL DAILY PAYMENTS AS NEGATIVE BARS ON THE Y-AXIS (DIVIDE DAILY DEPOSIT/PAYMENT BY THE SIZE OF A SQUARE TO FIND THE NUMBER OF SQUARES TO FILL)
- BUILD YOUR BALANCE LINE CHART USING YOUR DAILY BALANCE

MONTH:

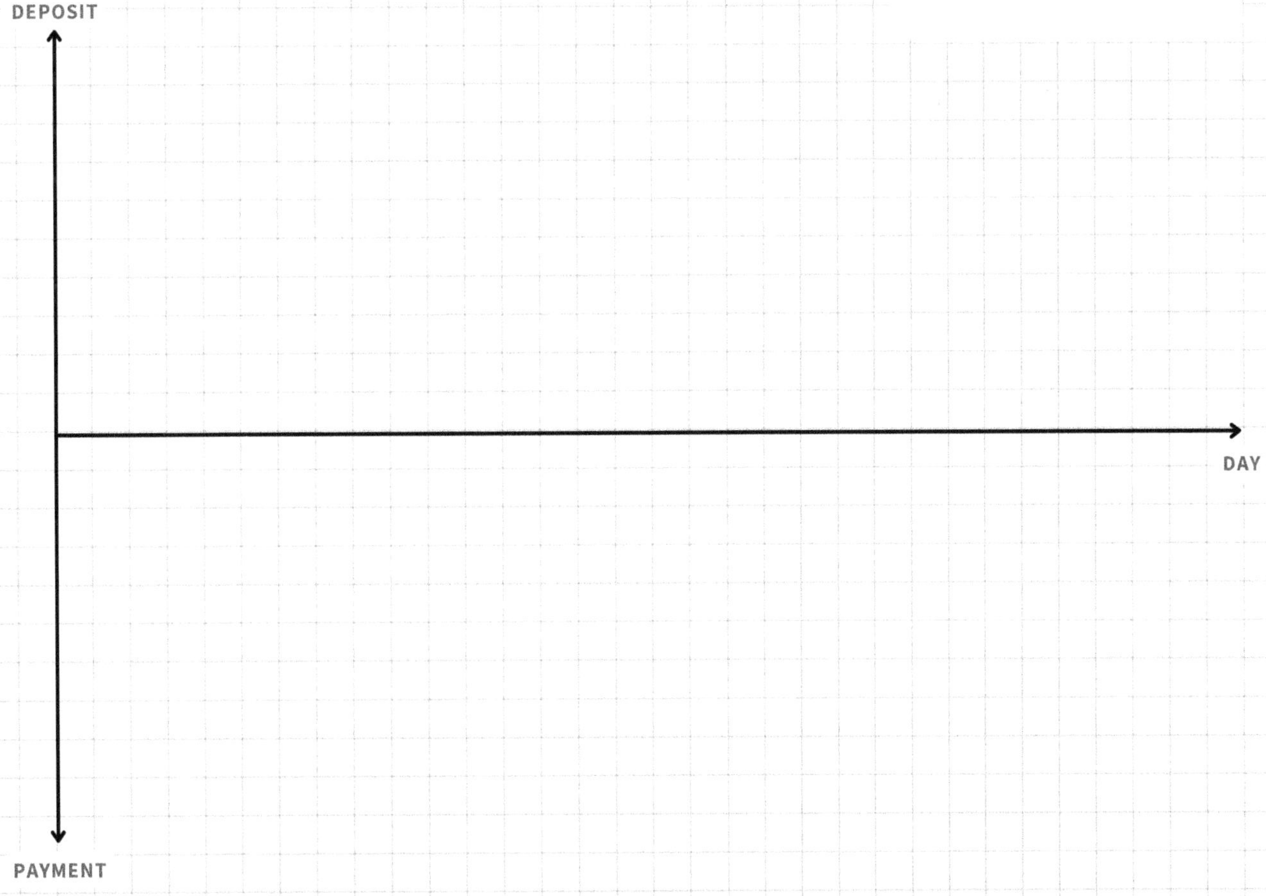

MONTHLY PAYMENTS & DEPOSITS

MONTH : ....

DATE	DAY	PAYMENT / DEBIT (-)	DEPOSIT / CREDIT (+)	BALANCE	NOTES
1					
2					
3					
4					
5					
6					
7					
8					
9					
10					
11					
12					
13					
14					
15					
16					
17					
18					
19					
20					
21					
22					
23					
24					
25					
26					
27					
28					
29					
30					
31					
TOTAL					

MONTHLY PAYMENTS & DEPOSITS CHART

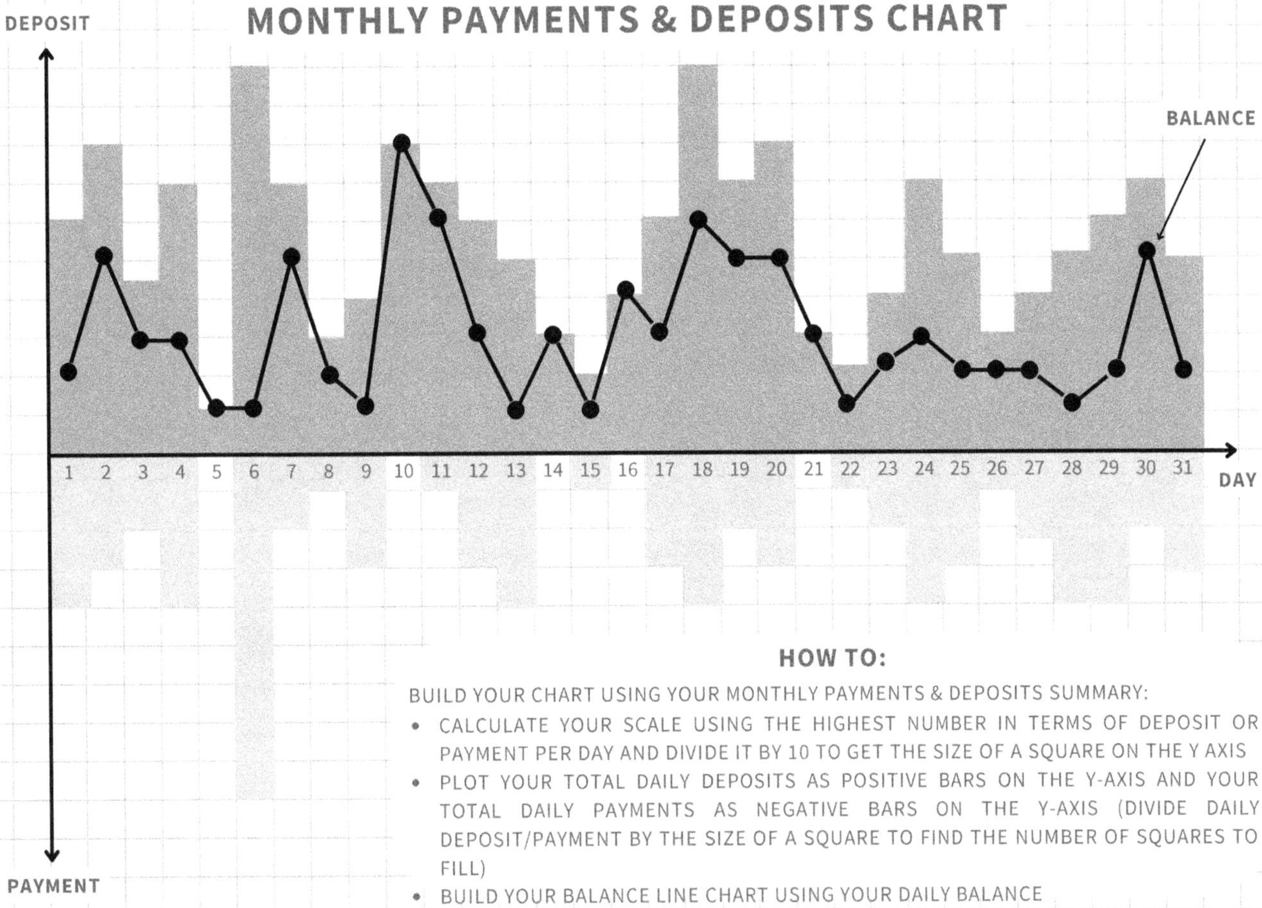

HOW TO:

BUILD YOUR CHART USING YOUR MONTHLY PAYMENTS & DEPOSITS SUMMARY:

- CALCULATE YOUR SCALE USING THE HIGHEST NUMBER IN TERMS OF DEPOSIT OR PAYMENT PER DAY AND DIVIDE IT BY 10 TO GET THE SIZE OF A SQUARE ON THE Y AXIS
- PLOT YOUR TOTAL DAILY DEPOSITS AS POSITIVE BARS ON THE Y-AXIS AND YOUR TOTAL DAILY PAYMENTS AS NEGATIVE BARS ON THE Y-AXIS (DIVIDE DAILY DEPOSIT/PAYMENT BY THE SIZE OF A SQUARE TO FIND THE NUMBER OF SQUARES TO FILL)
- BUILD YOUR BALANCE LINE CHART USING YOUR DAILY BALANCE

MONTH:

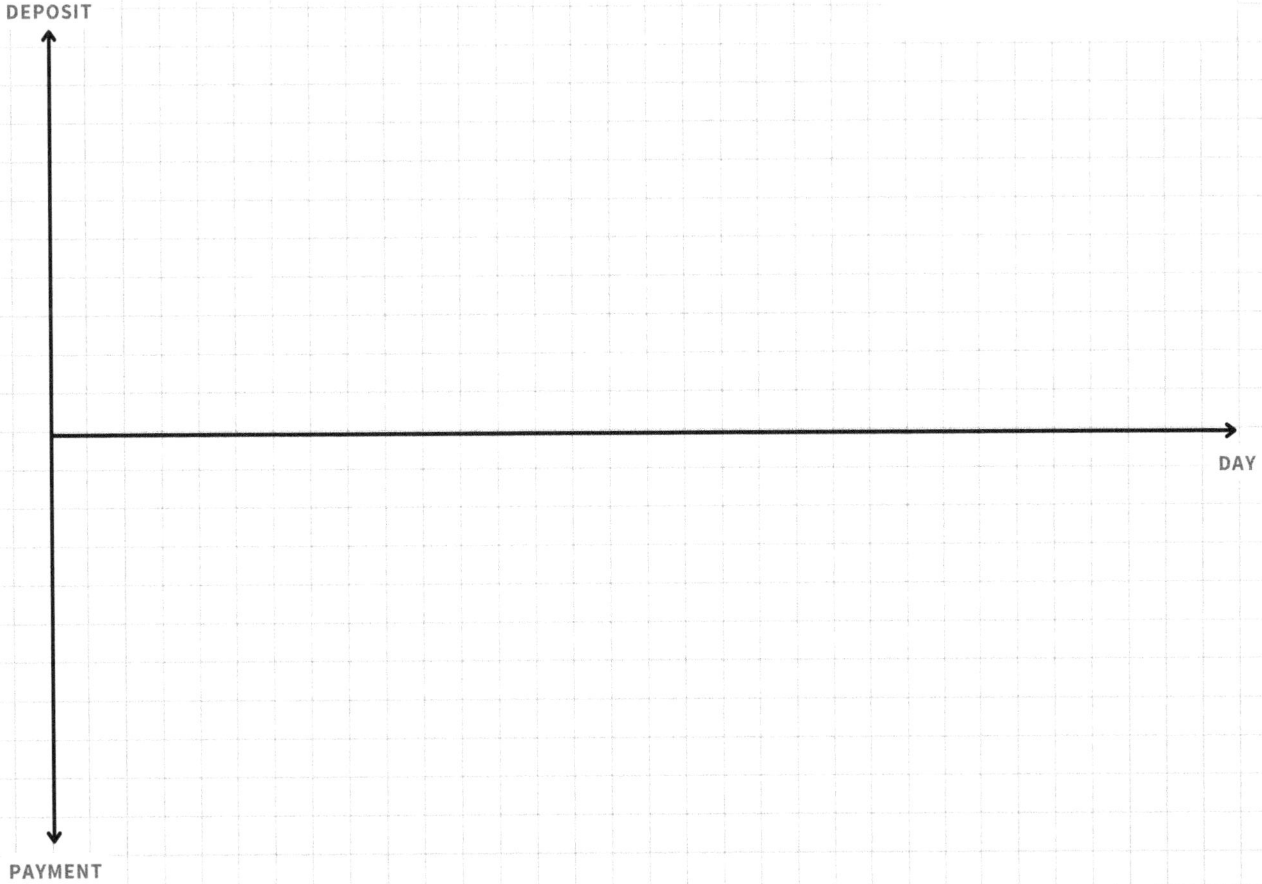

MONTHLY PAYMENTS & DEPOSITS

MONTH : ....

DATE	DAY	PAYMENT / DEBIT (-)	DEPOSIT / CREDIT (+)	BALANCE	NOTES
1					
2					
3					
4					
5					
6					
7					
8					
9					
10					
11					
12					
13					
14					
15					
16					
17					
18					
19					
20					
21					
22					
23					
24					
25					
26					
27					
28					
29					
30					
31					
TOTAL					

MONTHLY PAYMENTS & DEPOSITS CHART

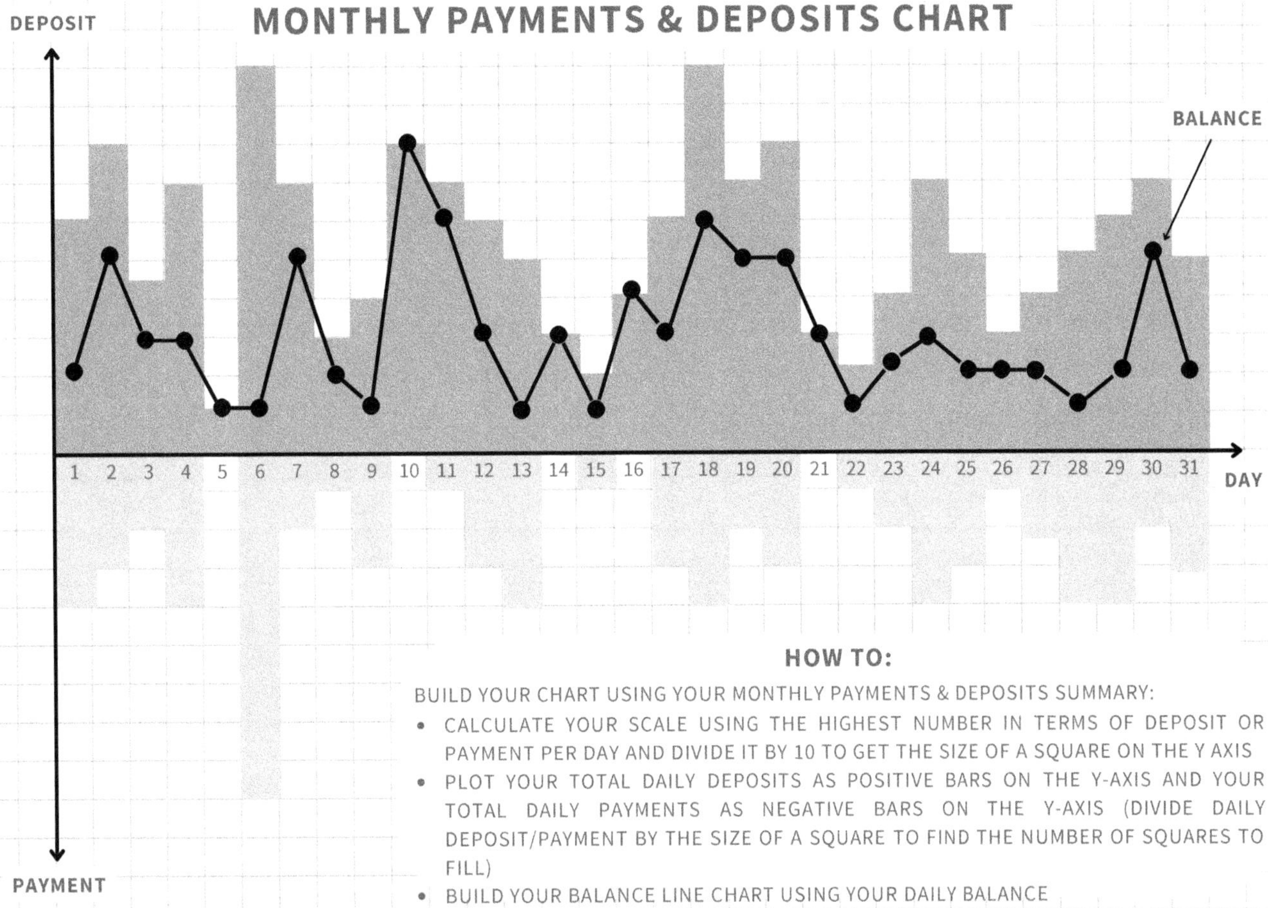

HOW TO:

BUILD YOUR CHART USING YOUR MONTHLY PAYMENTS & DEPOSITS SUMMARY:

- CALCULATE YOUR SCALE USING THE HIGHEST NUMBER IN TERMS OF DEPOSIT OR PAYMENT PER DAY AND DIVIDE IT BY 10 TO GET THE SIZE OF A SQUARE ON THE Y AXIS
- PLOT YOUR TOTAL DAILY DEPOSITS AS POSITIVE BARS ON THE Y-AXIS AND YOUR TOTAL DAILY PAYMENTS AS NEGATIVE BARS ON THE Y-AXIS (DIVIDE DAILY DEPOSIT/PAYMENT BY THE SIZE OF A SQUARE TO FIND THE NUMBER OF SQUARES TO FILL)
- BUILD YOUR BALANCE LINE CHART USING YOUR DAILY BALANCE

MONTH:

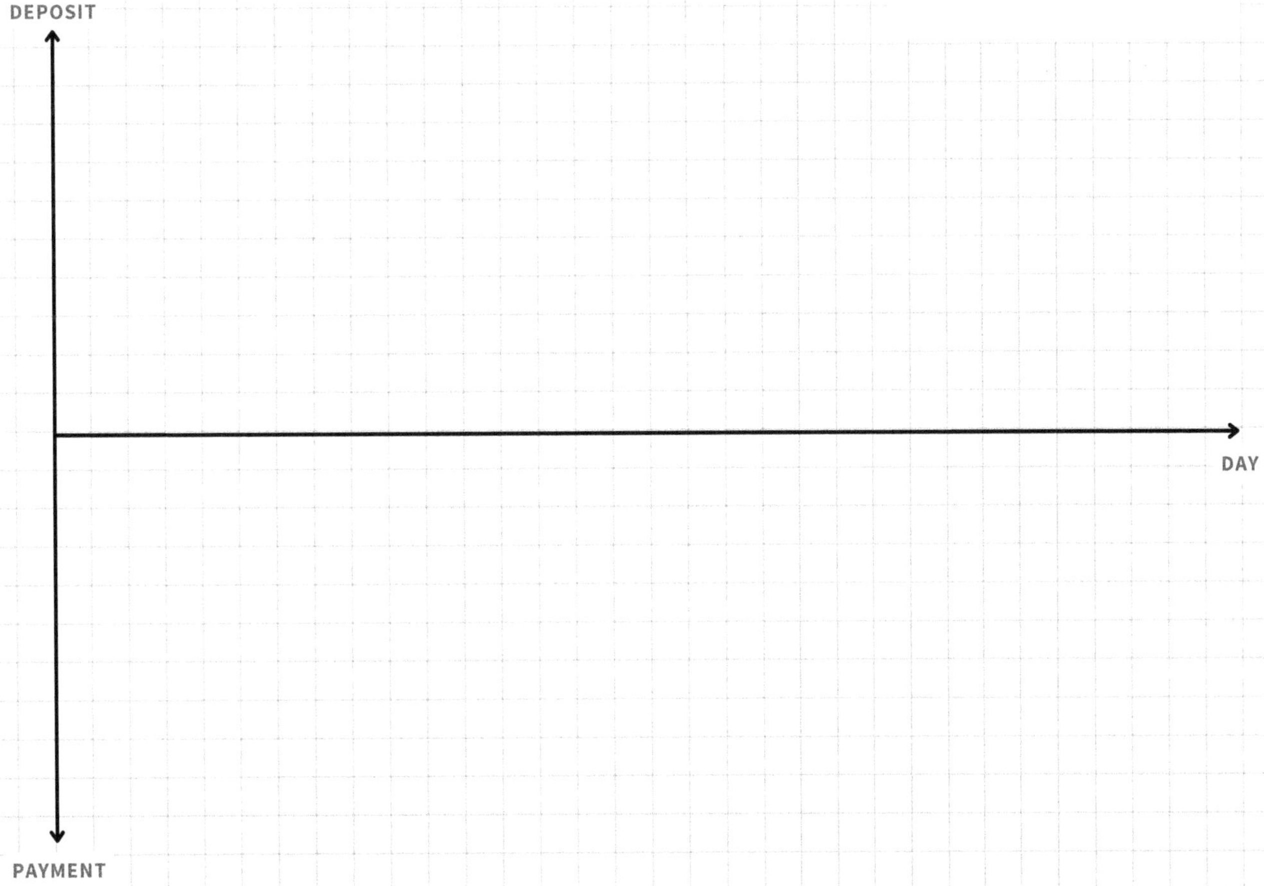

MONTHLY PAYMENTS & DEPOSITS

MONTH : ....

DATE	DAY	PAYMENT / DEBIT (-)	DEPOSIT / CREDIT (+)	BALANCE	NOTES
1					
2					
3					
4					
5					
6					
7					
8					
9					
10					
11					
12					
13					
14					
15					
16					
17					
18					
19					
20					
21					
22					
23					
24					
25					
26					
27					
28					
29					
30					
31					
TOTAL					

MONTHLY PAYMENTS & DEPOSITS CHART

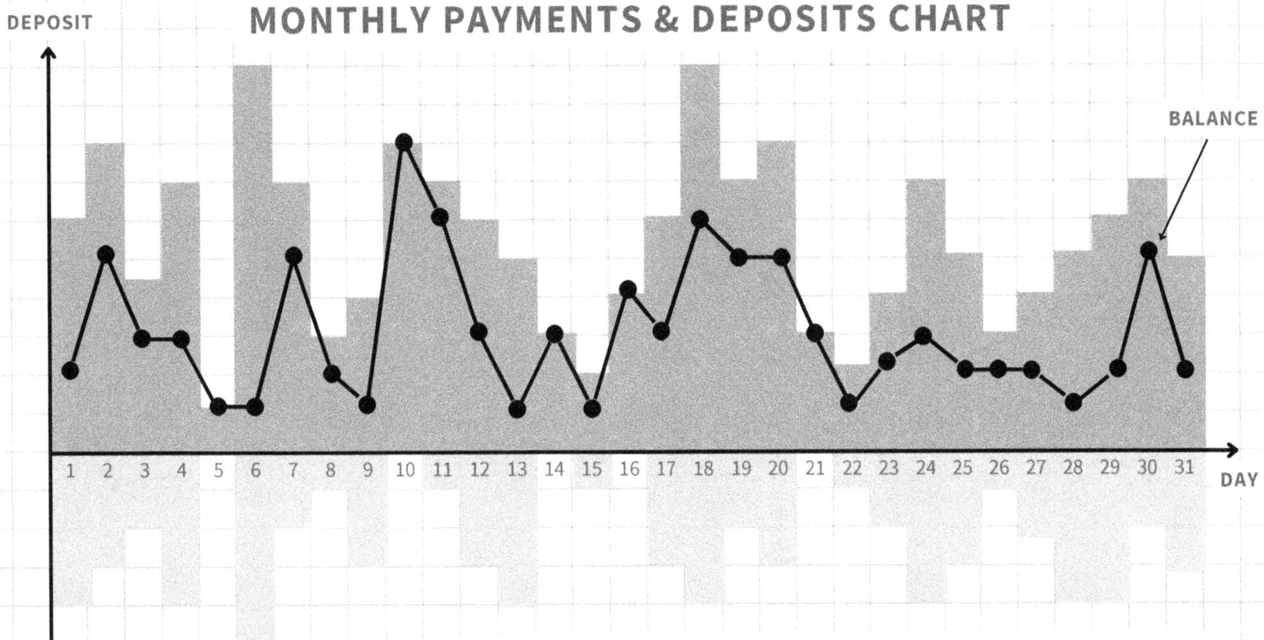

HOW TO:

BUILD YOUR CHART USING YOUR MONTHLY PAYMENTS & DEPOSITS SUMMARY:

- CALCULATE YOUR SCALE USING THE HIGHEST NUMBER IN TERMS OF DEPOSIT OR PAYMENT PER DAY AND DIVIDE IT BY 10 TO GET THE SIZE OF A SQUARE ON THE Y AXIS
- PLOT YOUR TOTAL DAILY DEPOSITS AS POSITIVE BARS ON THE Y-AXIS AND YOUR TOTAL DAILY PAYMENTS AS NEGATIVE BARS ON THE Y-AXIS (DIVIDE DAILY DEPOSIT/PAYMENT BY THE SIZE OF A SQUARE TO FIND THE NUMBER OF SQUARES TO FILL)
- BUILD YOUR BALANCE LINE CHART USING YOUR DAILY BALANCE

MONTH:

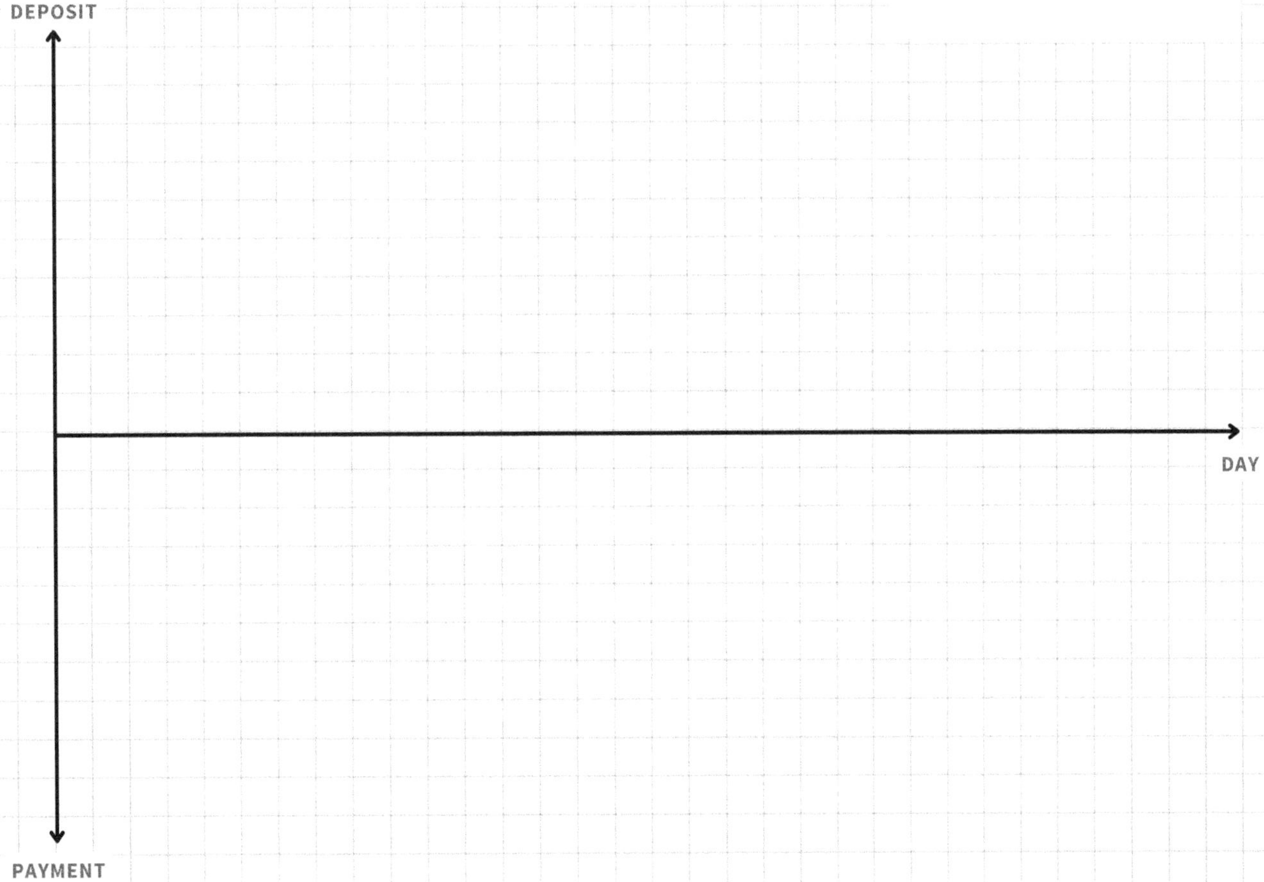

MONTHLY PAYMENTS & DEPOSITS

MONTH : ....

DATE	DAY	PAYMENT / DEBIT (-)	DEPOSIT / CREDIT (+)	BALANCE	NOTES
1					
2					
3					
4					
5					
6					
7					
8					
9					
10					
11					
12					
13					
14					
15					
16					
17					
18					
19					
20					
21					
22					
23					
24					
25					
26					
27					
28					
29					
30					
31					
TOTAL					

MONTHLY PAYMENTS & DEPOSITS CHART

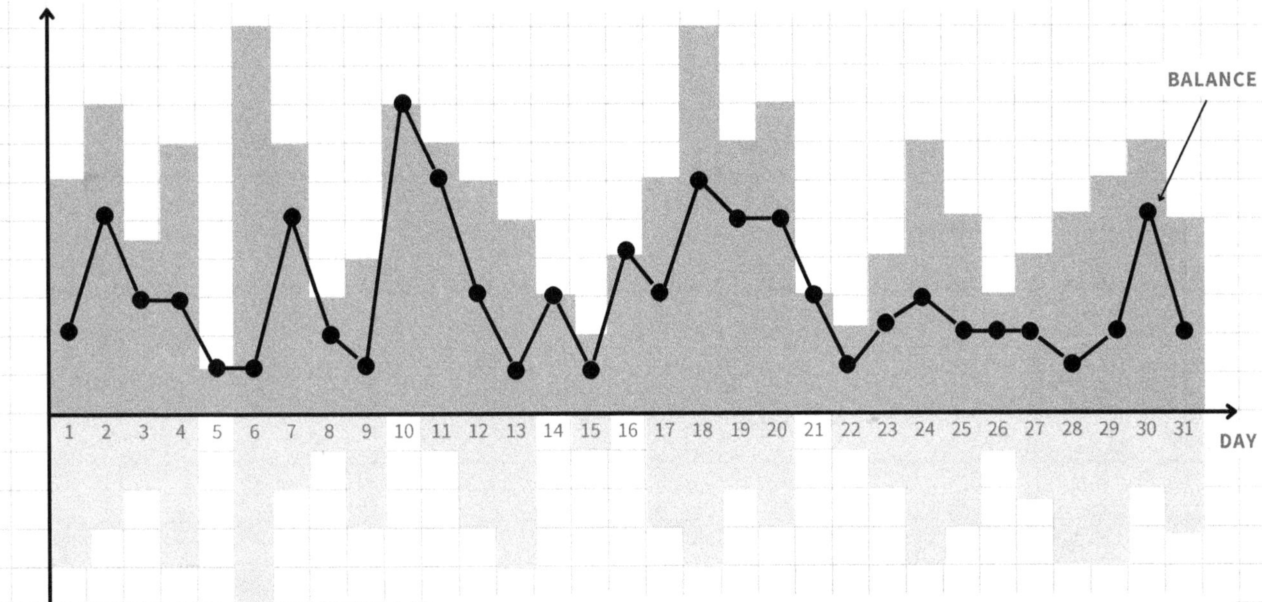

HOW TO:

BUILD YOUR CHART USING YOUR MONTHLY PAYMENTS & DEPOSITS SUMMARY:

- CALCULATE YOUR SCALE USING THE HIGHEST NUMBER IN TERMS OF DEPOSIT OR PAYMENT PER DAY AND DIVIDE IT BY 10 TO GET THE SIZE OF A SQUARE ON THE Y AXIS
- PLOT YOUR TOTAL DAILY DEPOSITS AS POSITIVE BARS ON THE Y-AXIS AND YOUR TOTAL DAILY PAYMENTS AS NEGATIVE BARS ON THE Y-AXIS (DIVIDE DAILY DEPOSIT/PAYMENT BY THE SIZE OF A SQUARE TO FIND THE NUMBER OF SQUARES TO FILL)
- BUILD YOUR BALANCE LINE CHART USING YOUR DAILY BALANCE

MONTH:

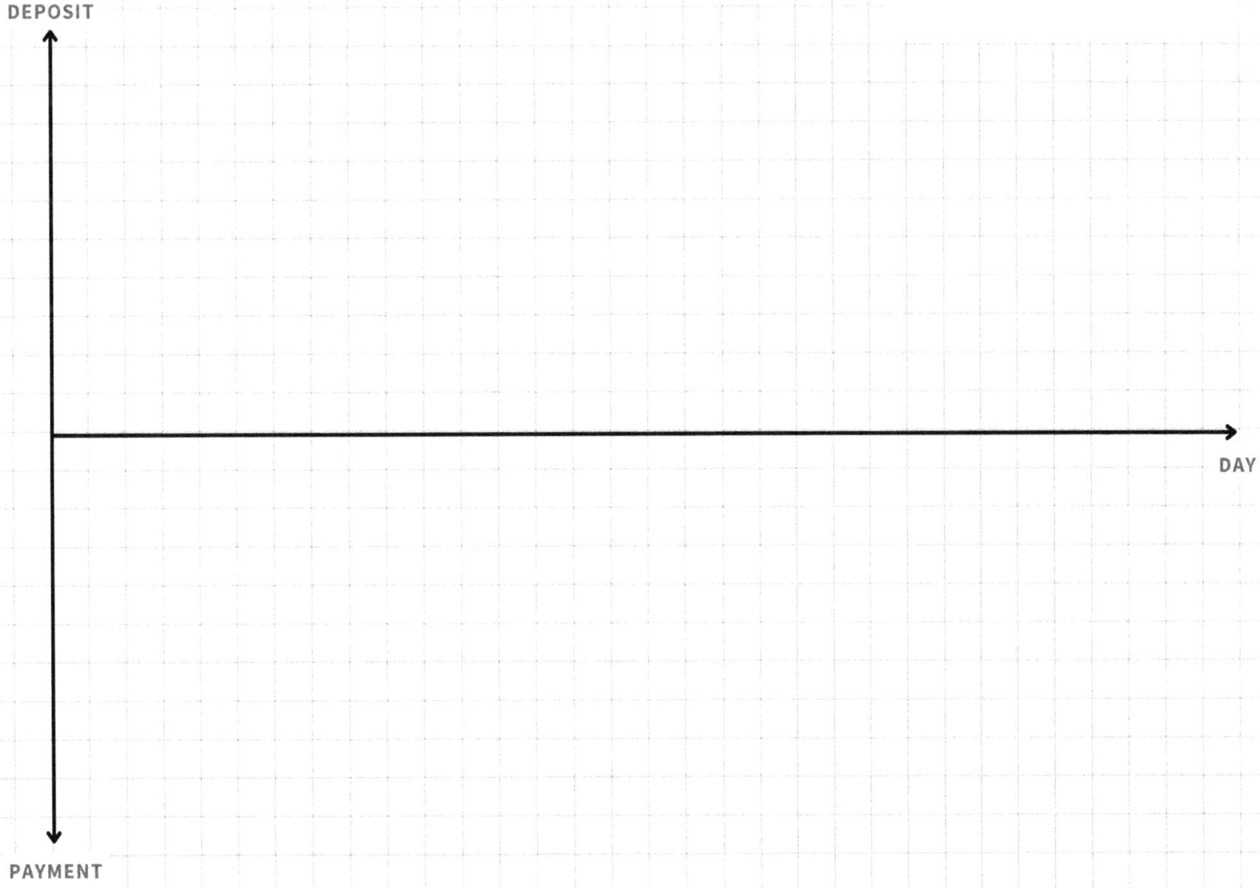

DAILY PAYMENTS & DEPOSITS

YEAR ....   BALANCE

CHECK #	DATE	DESCRIPTION	PAYMENT (-)	TAX	DEPOSIT (+)	✓	

DAILY PAYMENTS & DEPOSITS

YEAR ....

BALANCE

CHECK #	DATE	DESCRIPTION	PAYMENT (-)	TAX	DEPOSIT (+)	✓	

DAILY PAYMENTS & DEPOSITS

YEAR ....

BALANCE

CHECK #	DATE	DESCRIPTION	PAYMENT (-)	TAX	DEPOSIT (+)	✓	

DAILY PAYMENTS & DEPOSITS

YEAR ....   **BALANCE**

CHECK #	DATE	DESCRIPTION	PAYMENT (-)	TAX	DEPOSIT (+)	✓	

DAILY PAYMENTS & DEPOSITS

YEAR .... BALANCE

CHECK #	DATE	DESCRIPTION	PAYMENT (-)	TAX	DEPOSIT (+)	✓	

DAILY PAYMENTS & DEPOSITS

YEAR .... **BALANCE**

CHECK #	DATE	DESCRIPTION	PAYMENT (-)	TAX	DEPOSIT (+)	✓	

DAILY PAYMENTS & DEPOSITS

YEAR ....

BALANCE

CHECK #	DATE	DESCRIPTION	PAYMENT (-)	TAX	DEPOSIT (+)	✓	

DAILY PAYMENTS & DEPOSITS

YEAR .... BALANCE

CHECK #	DATE	DESCRIPTION	PAYMENT (-)	TAX	DEPOSIT (+)	✓	

DAILY PAYMENTS & DEPOSITS

YEAR ....

BALANCE

CHECK #	DATE	DESCRIPTION	PAYMENT (-)	TAX	DEPOSIT (+)	✓	

DAILY PAYMENTS & DEPOSITS

YEAR ....

BALANCE

CHECK #	DATE	DESCRIPTION	PAYMENT (-)	TAX	DEPOSIT (+)	✓	

DAILY PAYMENTS & DEPOSITS

YEAR ....

BALANCE

CHECK #	DATE	DESCRIPTION	PAYMENT (-)	TAX	DEPOSIT (+)	✓	

DAILY PAYMENTS & DEPOSITS

YEAR ....

BALANCE

CHECK #	DATE	DESCRIPTION	PAYMENT (-)	TAX	DEPOSIT (+)	✓	

DAILY PAYMENTS & DEPOSITS

YEAR ....

BALANCE

CHECK #	DATE	DESCRIPTION	PAYMENT (-)	TAX	DEPOSIT (+)	✓	

DAILY PAYMENTS & DEPOSITS

YEAR ....

BALANCE

CHECK #	DATE	DESCRIPTION	PAYMENT (-)	TAX	DEPOSIT (+)	✓	

DAILY PAYMENTS & DEPOSITS

YEAR ....   BALANCE

CHECK #	DATE	DESCRIPTION	PAYMENT (-)		TAX	DEPOSIT (+)		✓		

DAILY PAYMENTS & DEPOSITS

YEAR ....   BALANCE

CHECK #	DATE	DESCRIPTION	PAYMENT (-)	TAX	DEPOSIT (+)	✓	

DAILY PAYMENTS & DEPOSITS

YEAR ....

CHECK #	DATE	DESCRIPTION	PAYMENT (-)	TAX	DEPOSIT (+)	✓	BALANCE

DAILY PAYMENTS & DEPOSITS

YEAR ....

CHECK #	DATE	DESCRIPTION	PAYMENT (-)		TAX	DEPOSIT (+)		✓	BALANCE	

DAILY PAYMENTS & DEPOSITS

YEAR ....

BALANCE

CHECK #	DATE	DESCRIPTION	PAYMENT (-)	TAX	DEPOSIT (+)	✓	

DAILY PAYMENTS & DEPOSITS

YEAR .... **BALANCE**

CHECK #	DATE	DESCRIPTION	PAYMENT (-)	TAX	DEPOSIT (+)	✓	

DAILY PAYMENTS & DEPOSITS

YEAR ....

BALANCE

CHECK #	DATE	DESCRIPTION	PAYMENT (-)	TAX	DEPOSIT (+)	✓	

DAILY PAYMENTS & DEPOSITS

YEAR ....   BALANCE

CHECK #	DATE	DESCRIPTION	PAYMENT (-)	TAX	DEPOSIT (+)	✓	

DAILY PAYMENTS & DEPOSITS

YEAR ....

BALANCE

CHECK #	DATE	DESCRIPTION	PAYMENT (-)		TAX	DEPOSIT (+)		✓		

DAILY PAYMENTS & DEPOSITS

YEAR ....

CHECK #	DATE	DESCRIPTION	PAYMENT (-)	TAX	DEPOSIT (+)	✓	BALANCE

DAILY PAYMENTS & DEPOSITS

YEAR ....

CHECK #	DATE	DESCRIPTION	PAYMENT (-)	TAX	DEPOSIT (+)	✓	BALANCE

DAILY PAYMENTS & DEPOSITS

YEAR ....   BALANCE

CHECK #	DATE	DESCRIPTION	PAYMENT (-)	TAX	DEPOSIT (+)	✓	

DAILY PAYMENTS & DEPOSITS

YEAR .... BALANCE

CHECK #	DATE	DESCRIPTION	PAYMENT (-)		TAX	DEPOSIT (+)		✓		

DAILY PAYMENTS & DEPOSITS

YEAR ....   BALANCE

CHECK #	DATE	DESCRIPTION	PAYMENT (-)	TAX	DEPOSIT (+)	✓	

DAILY PAYMENTS & DEPOSITS

YEAR ....

BALANCE

CHECK #	DATE	DESCRIPTION	PAYMENT (-)	TAX	DEPOSIT (+)	✓	

DAILY PAYMENTS & DEPOSITS

YEAR ....   BALANCE

CHECK #	DATE	DESCRIPTION	PAYMENT (-)	TAX	DEPOSIT (+)	✓	

DAILY PAYMENTS & DEPOSITS

YEAR ....

BALANCE

CHECK #	DATE	DESCRIPTION	PAYMENT (-)		TAX	DEPOSIT (+)		✓		

DAILY PAYMENTS & DEPOSITS

YEAR ....   BALANCE

CHECK #	DATE	DESCRIPTION	PAYMENT (-)	TAX	DEPOSIT (+)	✓	

DAILY PAYMENTS & DEPOSITS

YEAR ....

BALANCE

CHECK #	DATE	DESCRIPTION	PAYMENT (-)	TAX	DEPOSIT (+)	✓	

DAILY PAYMENTS & DEPOSITS

YEAR ....

CHECK #	DATE	DESCRIPTION	PAYMENT (-)	TAX	DEPOSIT (+)	✓	BALANCE

DAILY PAYMENTS & DEPOSITS

YEAR ....

BALANCE

CHECK #	DATE	DESCRIPTION	PAYMENT (-)	TAX	DEPOSIT (+)	✓	

DAILY PAYMENTS & DEPOSITS

YEAR ....

BALANCE

CHECK #	DATE	DESCRIPTION	PAYMENT (-)	TAX	DEPOSIT (+)	✓	

DAILY PAYMENTS & DEPOSITS

YEAR ....

CHECK #	DATE	DESCRIPTION	PAYMENT (-)	TAX	DEPOSIT (+)	✓	BALANCE

DAILY PAYMENTS & DEPOSITS

YEAR ....   BALANCE

CHECK #	DATE	DESCRIPTION	PAYMENT (-)		TAX	DEPOSIT (+)		✓		

DAILY PAYMENTS & DEPOSITS

YEAR ....

CHECK #	DATE	DESCRIPTION	PAYMENT (-)	TAX	DEPOSIT (+)	✓	BALANCE

DAILY PAYMENTS & DEPOSITS

YEAR ....

CHECK #	DATE	DESCRIPTION	PAYMENT (-)	TAX	DEPOSIT (+)	✓	BALANCE

DAILY PAYMENTS & DEPOSITS

YEAR ....

CHECK #	DATE	DESCRIPTION	PAYMENT (-)	TAX	DEPOSIT (+)	✓	BALANCE

DAILY PAYMENTS & DEPOSITS

YEAR ....

CHECK #	DATE	DESCRIPTION	PAYMENT (-)	TAX	DEPOSIT (+)	✓	BALANCE

DAILY PAYMENTS & DEPOSITS

YEAR ....

BALANCE

CHECK #	DATE	DESCRIPTION	PAYMENT (-)	TAX	DEPOSIT (+)	✓	

DAILY PAYMENTS & DEPOSITS

YEAR ....

CHECK #	DATE	DESCRIPTION	PAYMENT (-)	TAX	DEPOSIT (+)	✓	BALANCE

DAILY PAYMENTS & DEPOSITS

YEAR ....

BALANCE

CHECK #	DATE	DESCRIPTION	PAYMENT (-)		TAX	DEPOSIT (+)		✓		

DAILY PAYMENTS & DEPOSITS

YEAR ....   BALANCE

CHECK #	DATE	DESCRIPTION	PAYMENT (-)	TAX	DEPOSIT (+)	✓	

DAILY PAYMENTS & DEPOSITS

YEAR ....

BALANCE

CHECK #	DATE	DESCRIPTION	PAYMENT (-)	TAX	DEPOSIT (+)	✓	

DAILY PAYMENTS & DEPOSITS

YEAR .... **BALANCE**

CHECK #	DATE	DESCRIPTION	PAYMENT (-)	TAX	DEPOSIT (+)	✓	

DAILY PAYMENTS & DEPOSITS

YEAR ....

BALANCE

CHECK #	DATE	DESCRIPTION	PAYMENT (-)	TAX	DEPOSIT (+)	✓	

DAILY PAYMENTS & DEPOSITS

YEAR .... BALANCE

CHECK #	DATE	DESCRIPTION	PAYMENT (-)	TAX	DEPOSIT (+)	✓	

DAILY PAYMENTS & DEPOSITS

YEAR ....

BALANCE

CHECK #	DATE	DESCRIPTION	PAYMENT (-)		TAX	DEPOSIT (+)		✓		

DAILY PAYMENTS & DEPOSITS

YEAR ....   BALANCE

CHECK #	DATE	DESCRIPTION	PAYMENT (-)	TAX	DEPOSIT (+)	✓	

DAILY PAYMENTS & DEPOSITS

YEAR ....

BALANCE

CHECK #	DATE	DESCRIPTION	PAYMENT (-)	TAX	DEPOSIT (+)	✓	

DAILY PAYMENTS & DEPOSITS

YEAR ....   BALANCE

CHECK #	DATE	DESCRIPTION	PAYMENT (-)	TAX	DEPOSIT (+)	✓	

DAILY PAYMENTS & DEPOSITS

YEAR .... BALANCE

CHECK #	DATE	DESCRIPTION	PAYMENT (-)	TAX	DEPOSIT (+)	✓	

DAILY PAYMENTS & DEPOSITS

YEAR ....

CHECK #	DATE	DESCRIPTION	PAYMENT (-)	TAX	DEPOSIT (+)	✓	BALANCE

DAILY PAYMENTS & DEPOSITS

YEAR ....

BALANCE

CHECK #	DATE	DESCRIPTION	PAYMENT (-)	TAX	DEPOSIT (+)	✓	

DAILY PAYMENTS & DEPOSITS

YEAR ....

CHECK #	DATE	DESCRIPTION	PAYMENT (-)	TAX	DEPOSIT (+)	✓	BALANCE

DAILY PAYMENTS & DEPOSITS

YEAR ....

BALANCE

CHECK #	DATE	DESCRIPTION	PAYMENT (-)	TAX	DEPOSIT (+)	✓	

DAILY PAYMENTS & DEPOSITS

YEAR ....

CHECK #	DATE	DESCRIPTION	PAYMENT (-)	TAX	DEPOSIT (+)	✓	BALANCE

DAILY PAYMENTS & DEPOSITS

YEAR ....

CHECK #	DATE	DESCRIPTION	PAYMENT (-)	TAX	DEPOSIT (+)	✓	BALANCE

DAILY PAYMENTS & DEPOSITS

YEAR .... **BALANCE**

CHECK #	DATE	DESCRIPTION	PAYMENT (-)	TAX	DEPOSIT (+)	✓	

DAILY PAYMENTS & DEPOSITS

YEAR ....

BALANCE

CHECK #	DATE	DESCRIPTION	PAYMENT (-)	TAX	DEPOSIT (+)	✓	

DAILY PAYMENTS & DEPOSITS

YEAR ....

BALANCE

CHECK #	DATE	DESCRIPTION	PAYMENT (-)	TAX	DEPOSIT (+)	✓	

DAILY PAYMENTS & DEPOSITS

YEAR ....

CHECK #	DATE	DESCRIPTION	PAYMENT (-)	TAX	DEPOSIT (+)	✓	BALANCE

DAILY PAYMENTS & DEPOSITS

YEAR .... BALANCE

CHECK #	DATE	DESCRIPTION	PAYMENT (-)	TAX	DEPOSIT (+)	✓	

DAILY PAYMENTS & DEPOSITS

YEAR ....

BALANCE

CHECK #	DATE	DESCRIPTION	PAYMENT (-)	TAX	DEPOSIT (+)	✓	

DAILY PAYMENTS & DEPOSITS

YEAR .... **BALANCE**

CHECK #	DATE	DESCRIPTION	PAYMENT (-)	TAX	DEPOSIT (+)	✓	

DAILY PAYMENTS & DEPOSITS

YEAR ....

BALANCE

CHECK #	DATE	DESCRIPTION	PAYMENT (-)	TAX	DEPOSIT (+)	✓	

DAILY PAYMENTS & DEPOSITS

YEAR ....

CHECK #	DATE	DESCRIPTION	PAYMENT (-)	TAX	DEPOSIT (+)	✓	BALANCE

DAILY PAYMENTS & DEPOSITS

YEAR ....

BALANCE

CHECK #	DATE	DESCRIPTION	PAYMENT (-)	TAX	DEPOSIT (+)	✓	

DAILY PAYMENTS & DEPOSITS

YEAR .... BALANCE

CHECK #	DATE	DESCRIPTION	PAYMENT (-)	TAX	DEPOSIT (+)	✓	

DAILY PAYMENTS & DEPOSITS

YEAR .... BALANCE

CHECK #	DATE	DESCRIPTION	PAYMENT (-)	TAX	DEPOSIT (+)	✓	

DAILY PAYMENTS & DEPOSITS

YEAR ....

BALANCE

CHECK #	DATE	DESCRIPTION	PAYMENT (-)	TAX	DEPOSIT (+)	✓	

DAILY PAYMENTS & DEPOSITS

YEAR ....

BALANCE

CHECK #	DATE	DESCRIPTION	PAYMENT (-)	TAX	DEPOSIT (+)	✓	

DAILY PAYMENTS & DEPOSITS

YEAR ....

CHECK #	DATE	DESCRIPTION	PAYMENT (-)	TAX	DEPOSIT (+)	✓	BALANCE

DAILY PAYMENTS & DEPOSITS

YEAR ....

BALANCE

CHECK #	DATE	DESCRIPTION	PAYMENT (-)	TAX	DEPOSIT (+)	✓	

DAILY PAYMENTS & DEPOSITS

YEAR ....

CHECK #	DATE	DESCRIPTION	PAYMENT (-)	TAX	DEPOSIT (+)	✓	BALANCE

DAILY PAYMENTS & DEPOSITS

YEAR ....

BALANCE

CHECK #	DATE	DESCRIPTION	PAYMENT (-)	TAX	DEPOSIT (+)	✓	

DAILY PAYMENTS & DEPOSITS

YEAR ....

CHECK #	DATE	DESCRIPTION	PAYMENT (-)	TAX	DEPOSIT (+)	✓	BALANCE

DAILY PAYMENTS & DEPOSITS

YEAR ....

BALANCE

CHECK #	DATE	DESCRIPTION	PAYMENT (-)		TAX	DEPOSIT (+)		✓		

DAILY PAYMENTS & DEPOSITS

YEAR ....

CHECK #	DATE	DESCRIPTION	PAYMENT (-)	TAX	DEPOSIT (+)	✓	BALANCE

DAILY PAYMENTS & DEPOSITS

YEAR .... BALANCE

CHECK #	DATE	DESCRIPTION	PAYMENT (-)	TAX	DEPOSIT (+)	✓	

DAILY PAYMENTS & DEPOSITS

YEAR ....

BALANCE

CHECK #	DATE	DESCRIPTION	PAYMENT (-)	TAX	DEPOSIT (+)	✓	

DAILY PAYMENTS & DEPOSITS

YEAR .... BALANCE

CHECK #	DATE	DESCRIPTION	PAYMENT (-)	TAX	DEPOSIT (+)	✓	

DAILY PAYMENTS & DEPOSITS

YEAR ....

BALANCE

CHECK #	DATE	DESCRIPTION	PAYMENT (-)	TAX	DEPOSIT (+)	✓	

DAILY PAYMENTS & DEPOSITS

YEAR ....

CHECK #	DATE	DESCRIPTION	PAYMENT (-)	TAX	DEPOSIT (+)	✓	BALANCE

DAILY PAYMENTS & DEPOSITS

YEAR ....

CHECK #	DATE	DESCRIPTION	PAYMENT (-)		TAX	DEPOSIT (+)		✓	BALANCE	

DAILY PAYMENTS & DEPOSITS

YEAR ....

BALANCE

CHECK #	DATE	DESCRIPTION	PAYMENT (-)	TAX	DEPOSIT (+)	✓	

DAILY PAYMENTS & DEPOSITS

YEAR ....

CHECK #	DATE	DESCRIPTION	PAYMENT (-)	TAX	DEPOSIT (+)	✓	BALANCE

DAILY PAYMENTS & DEPOSITS

YEAR ....

BALANCE

CHECK #	DATE	DESCRIPTION	PAYMENT (-)		TAX	DEPOSIT (+)		✓		

www.ingramcontent.com/pod-product-compliance
Lightning Source LLC
Chambersburg PA
CBHW051757200326
41597CB00025B/4595
* 9 7 8 1 8 0 3 9 3 2 1 9 4 *